Taming the RESTLESS MIND

Winning tips unfolded

rashmi singh

PUSTAK MAHAL®

Published by
Pustak Mahal®, Delhi
J-3/16, Daryaganj, New Delhi-110002
☎ 23276539, 23272783, 23272784 • *Fax:* 011-23260518
E-mail: info@pustakmahal.com • *Website:* www.pustakmahal.com

Sales Centre
• 10-B, Netaji Subhash Marg, Daryaganj, New Delhi-110002
☎ 23268292, 23268293, 23279900 • *Fax:* 011-23280567
E-mail: rapidexdelhi@indiatimes.com

• 6686, Khari Baoli, Delhi-110006
☎ 23944314, 23911979

Branches
Bengaluru: ☎ 080-22234025 • *Telefax:* 080-22240209
E-mail: pustak@airtelmail.in • pustak@sancharnet.in
Mumbai: ☎ 022-22010941, 022-22053387
E-mail: rapidex@bom5.vsnl.net.in
Patna: ☎ 0612-3294193 • *Telefax:* 0612-2302719
E-mail: rapidexptn@rediffmail.com
Hyderabad: *Telefax:* 040-24737290
E-mail: pustakmahalhyd@yahoo.co.in

ISBN 978-81-223-1267-6
Edition : 2012

Printed at : Param Offsetters, Okhla, New Delhi-110020

Praise for previous work : Love's Journey

ECONOMIC TIMES CASUAL'S (epaper) REVIEW:

rack of reads

A PRISTINE SURMISE

RASHMI SINGHS BOOK LOVES JOURNEY DEPICTS LIFE THROUGH ALL ITS MURK AND FILTH ONLY TO INSTILL FAITH IN THE GOOD

DEBOLINA SEN

Depicting the life of a woman who dreams of true love, Rashmi Singh has knitted a story which talks of faith and distrust in the same breath. Build around the character Jennifer Sebastian, the book is an unusual saga of belief in God and true love that takes the readers through a whirlwind of events which are interspersed with hatred, greed, sex and compromises. The blend of good and evil, dreams and reality, hope and fate makes the novel a complete read that projects life through its true colours.

AT A BLOG: Track2media

July 10, 2011

What makes *Love's Journey* worth reading is the fact that the story line seems to have been drawn from the real life. Rashmi Singh as a debutant writer has shown tremendous conviction in narrating the cruel face of society without getting judgmental or taking up advocacy.

Unlike many other novelists who get carried by their protagonists and characterization gets into either black or white, Rashmi Singh doesn't fail to see that grey shades are there in the real world. Every sinner has a past and beasts too can have a soft side—a fact that Love's Journey finds in some otherwise manipulative characters like the film director Shambhu Vasan.

May be the feminine instinct in Rashmi Singh was always ahead of the writer's instinct to do justice with the lead character. After all, only a woman with no undue baggage of advocacy can understand that howsoever successful a woman may be, she still needs an anchor, a male companion deep in her dreams. So did Jennifer, even though her journey was dictated by the destiny and went through poverty and cruelty.

Review of a customer Ayushree Nandan at Flipkart:

A Breathtaking piece hits the market!

THIS BOOK DOESN'T ONLY SPEAK FOR THE LADIES IN TODAY'S FAST-PACE, MATERIALISTIC AND COLD-BLOODED WORLD WHO BREATHE FOR TRUE LOVE, BUT ALSO SPEAKS FOR THE HUMANITY AS A WHOLE. It is one book which will make you all question yourselves again and again and again about you being born as a Human Being in this world! Are we so indulge in our businesses, that we have forgotten that we are human beings and it is our duty to respect Humanity?

This is the story of this Jenny Girl who would make your minds go bewildered and make you realize that HUMANITY IS BEING DISRESPECTED BUT IT IS NECESSARY TO MAKE IT BLOOM AGAIN IN THIS VAST PIECE OF EARTH.

Love's Journey literally made me cry by the end of 'my journey' of reading the book. Reading it is a 'MUST' for EVERYONE WHO IS OR WANTS TO BE HUMANE. And please for God's sake if you're like one of those Bloody Jerks who know nothing but to become a pain in the asses for 'human beings' like Jenny, this Book isn't meant for you Dirty Little Losers!!!

Humanity is God's Garden, fellas.

Don't let the Devil play in it!

Well I cherished the book. Thumbs Up from my side! :)

Love's Journey

[224]

I liked the book, so calmly written the journey and hardships of women. Its shows different phases of the woman. The author has used perfect words to describe and elaborate the book. Its very interesting to read. "You never know about your fate," is what the book says.

Date Added: 07/28/2011 by Namrata Kejriwal

Acknowledgements & Thanks

My kind Baba, Rai Bahadur Panchanand Sharan Singh
My Daadi, Padmavati Devi – My Royal Dreaded Idol
Papa, Sri D.P. Singh; Ma, Shanti Devi
Father-in-law, Sri B.N. Singh;
Mother-in-law, Prem Lata Singh
Apurva, Ayushree – My lifelines
Amod Kumar – My husband
Bhaiya, S.K. Singh, Bhabhi, Anita Singh –
for encouraging me always

Rohit Gupta, CEO, Pustak Mahal,
for once again showing trust in me
after giving a successful launch pad
with Love's Journey

My friends, students and above all – God
Thank You All

P.S: Special thanks to my 'FAITH ' for always
making me to stand after a 'fall'

Author's Note

I know that life is very unpredictable and unkind to millions – especially when you compare yourself with others. But life comes to us in a way it has to come. It is we who have to mould and live it gracefully and successfully. Comparison leads to the wastage of this beautiful life which comes to us only once! Working as a Counsellor and Personality Development Trainer, I have known that there are times when you find yourself in a hot soup as you cannot discuss your problems even with your close friends.

This book is a sincere and honest attempt to discuss many such topics in an interesting and an enlightened way. Success does not mean that one should be excellent only at his workplace. It comprises of many essential ingredients of life which makes one a 'Winner' in every sense. This book will be a great help to all those who really want to bring in a change in their present existence and want to emerge as a winner on the platform called life.

If you have any query about life you may contact me at **rrashmi211@gmail.com** or at **http://www.facebook.com/Rashmii.S**

Preface

'Life is not what we get, it is how we mould and perceive it'.

No one can be a better expounder than me who was just a graduate, married early, bore a child, sank into a mucky slimy black ocean of unfulfilled cravings, desires, wants and dreams but moved ahead even after repeated setbacks – on the pedestal of Educational cushioning opening ways to luminous but hidden world.

I do not want to unfold the pages of the bygone phase of my life and beg unnecessary sympathies but just want to warn, and invigorate those who have sunk deep into the pool of depression and inferiority complex marring their personalities and life, brooding over the no-exit position of their gloomy catacombs.

The fatal efforts by the present youth to prove themselves physically, sexually and monetarily superior to others these days, has proved disastrous.

Taming the Restless Mind will help the readers to add the missing pinch of salt in their lives and to pave a successful and secure path for themselves.

We have heard of the past life and its regressions but how many of us can claim its authenticity and say with a definition about 'rebirths'? Life is the most unusual phenomenon gifted to us by the Supreme Creator. We get one life, and it is we who have to decide that we don't leave it longing!

Contents

[CHAPTER ONE]

THE MOST WANTED PHENOMENON

CONFIDENCE FACTOR

COME OUT OF THE SHYNESS SHELL: INSTILL SELF-ESTEEM

"You must love yourself before you love another. By accepting yourself AND fully being what you are, your simple presence can make others happy as well as keep you happy too".

Confidence in a person can only be instilled if he has SELF-ESTEEM – If he considers himself of some worth. We can say Self-Worth is the most important ingredient of Self-Esteem which in turn plays an important part in enhancing confidence in a person. Honour and respect are the urgent need of human existence or we can say they are the borne needs – the more self-esteem you get, the more inspired you are! Getting inspired means YOU ARE POSITIVELY MOTIVATED and if you are positively motivated, your energies are positively channelised which in turn leads to the enhancement of your confidence-level.

Winning Trick 1

STOP UNNECESSARY COMPARISON:

Confidence generates energies to respect and accept ourselves the way we are. Here I do not mean that people indulging in negative acts like criminals, etc should take pride in their work. What I mean is, those not so well-gifted naturally should STOP COMPARING THEMSELVES to their peers and should avoid unnecessary stress which might ruin their life and relationships.

Winning Trick 2

CONFIDENCE GENERATES SELF-RESPECT: IT ALL MATTERS IN HOW YOU SEE YOURSELF

Don't place your mistakes over your head as their weight might crush you. Instead, place them under your feet to make a platform to view your horizons.

So if we have confidence we will respect ourselves and if we respect ourselves we can respect the entire humanity, improve our relationships which can directly or indirectly lead to "achievements – small or big" leading to an increase in our happiness level!

Winning Trick 3

COME OUT OF YOUR SHYNESS SHELL

The Braggers Baggage:

I would like to stress upon a VERY IMPORTANT POINT. Some people are extremely shy but are great achievers but this "shyness" of theirs doesn't get them their deserved position. The braggers take away all the credit! Such people sometimes want to come out with their points and make known their accomplishments to others but the braggers or we can say the bullies very cunningly thwart their confidence hogging away all the limelight and appreciation.

TO SUCH PEOPLE I WANT TO MAKE A WAKE UP CALL – DON'T LET YOUR CREDITS BE EATEN BY SOMEONE ELSE. It is high time you realise your worth and very pleasantly speak your mind. I know the shy ones can ask me "HOW"? To them, my advice is to start their acts among their friend circle or family members because the shy ones are bullied or thwarted everywhere! Or say you can start 'A DUMMY CONVERSATION' in front of the mirror first.

Winning Trick 4

MARKET YOURSELF

Learn to market yourself. In this cut-throat competitive world, learn to make your achievements known. At times some people might laugh at you – disparage you but don't forget "THEY ARE THE JEALOUS ONES". YOU HAVE TO BECOME YOUR OWN ADVERTISING NETWORK AND WHY FEEL SHY ABOUT IT? People going in for Elections, Educational Institutions and even the Government are propagating their achievements!

Take a simple example, how would we come to know which commodity say toothpaste is available and meets our requirements if proper advertisement is not done for it – SAME WAY WE HAVE TO MARKET AND FEND FOR OURSELVES – THE COMPANIES HAVE SOURCES TO ADVERTISE AND WE SHOULD HAVE SELF-ESTEEM TO DO SO. However in doing so we must avoid self-praise or being OVER-CONFIDENT otherwise there will not be any difference between you and a 'bragger'. Like low self-esteem, over confidence too must be shunned. VANITY AND TOO MUCH PRIDE CAN BE RUINOUS.

FEAR OF FAILURE AND LACK OF CONCENTRATION

Fear of failure too eats or gnaws away ones confidence. Always fearing of not succeeding leads you nowhere.

Winning Trick 5

We should not forget that "FAILURE AND SUCCESS GO HAND IN HAND". If you are unsuccessful for once or even twice, it doesn't mean that you are worthless. This fear leads to LACK OF CONCENTRATION IN WORK AND STUDIES – THE CONSEQUENCES OF WHICH ARE SOMETIMES MURKEY AND DANGEROUS.

Winning Trick 6

We all are blessed with some quality or other, the only thing required is to harness 'the qualities' embedded in our personalities. We have seen the most pleasant looking person suffering from low self-esteem AND the not so good looking ones being the centre of attraction – so IT ALL DEPENDS HOW YOU TREAT YOURSELF AND YOUR PERCEPTION OF LIFE AND UNLIMITED OPPORTUNITIES BUDDING OUT OF IT!

Gift Hamper Of Winning Tricks:

EFFORTS AND STEPS TO INCREASE SELF-CONFIDENCE:

Here I would like to present a few points which can help people from all walks of society, age-groups and stream to gain confidence to give requisite lift to their spirits.

1. Have faith in yourself.
2. Respect and accept yourself as you are.
3. Hone and Polish your skills.
4. Let not fear of failure deter you from your aim.
5. If you fail, then you are made for 'other things in life'.
6. Enhancing personality is an on-going process – learn from every little incident.
7. Be well-informed. Read well.

8. Never underestimate yourself. If you have achieved anything, let the world know. Do this pleasantly.
9. Don't keep to your shell.
10. Try making friends. Socialize, but in a limit.
11. Be positive and humane but at the same to me safeguard your own interests too.
12. Fix your priorities in life. Don't be disparaged or insulted uselessly as some people derive pleasure while doing so.
13. LIFE IS ALWAYS NOT THE WAY WE DESIRE OR WANT. DO NOT LET NEGATIVE SITUATIONS MAR YOUR SELF-ESTEEM.

SO GET UP PULL YOURSELF AND FACE THE WORLD – REMEMBER NO ONE IS PERFECT. EVEN THE GODS HAD WEAKNESSES AND WEAK POINTS!

[CHAPTER TWO]

PAY PACKAGE RACE

THE UNHEALTHIEST COMPETITION

Nitpicks Of Job Factor

Another serious matter which I have often come across is the everyday increasing talk of 'Pay Packages'.

What I have noticed, 'the pay package syndrome' has come out of the classrooms of the students, floating through their Mess, Common Rooms, Hostels to the kitchens of their mothers and workplaces of their fathers.

Earlier only the students were bothered about their packages: to excel – to gain – to have an upper hand over their peers but now it seems even the workers of their houses know about their success or failures (regarding the 'Pay Packages' offered to them).

This phenomenon – to get better pay packages than their peers or rather the best pay package has made so many talented students to perish. Actually this pressure is not so easy to handle as easily I am putting it down and those who have undergone or undergoing will definitely agree.

Two – Sided Consequence:

This quest to have more doesn't stop at the point where students get their first pay package selected through Campus, but goes on increasing with each passing day – with each changing job.

This mounting pressure to get a lucrative pay package, gnaws away the hearts and minds of the youth. It has a TWO – SIDED CONSEQUENCE – either the pressure to get more in their lives drowns them in pools of depression where they end up ruining or damaging their physical and mental health respectively or make them robots, devoid of any feeling, cutting throats of their competitors to get more! Both the phenomena are frightening and damaging to the health of the present generation.

Parental Pressure:

Parents are equally to be blamed. Their hopes and aspirations are not only contained to the successful entry of their children in good institutes, but goes on burgeoning with every passing day! Pay Packages of their ward have become an element of status symbol in their social circle. Comparison of their child's package with other children and flaunting it if better than others, gives them unlimited mental satisfaction. In all this they forget that they are becoming a fillip in blowing off their child's entire life. The child, too unknowingly, to please his/her guardians sometimes tells lies or starts running away from life, breaking on the way.

Peer Pressure:

The most dangerous competition is one the Youth himself devises – that is, to get a better pay package than his friends, to enhance his image amongst his friends and most importantly among the girls who look for 'successful boys' as their boyfriends, without realizing that it is leading them to 'Mental Demolition'. During the initial years of college, it is the 'Macho Image' which matters the most to them but as the students reach their finals, everything suddenly starts revolving round 'Pay Packages'. This syndrome, which is not so seriously discussed these days, I am sure, is going to take a very serious form in years to come.

ADVICE AND WINNING TRICKS TO COMBAT JOB STRESS

Problems caused by your 'Jobs' and 'Pay Packages' can have a negative effect on your personal life. They can harm your relationships with family and friends and cause sleeplessness, depression and a variety of health problems.

Your emotions are contagious, and stress has an impact on the quality of your interactions with others. The better you are at managing your own stress, the more you'll positively affect those around you, and the less other people's stress will negatively affect you.

So it is very important for the youth in general to manage stress incurring both from 'Pay Package Syndrome' or 'Job Jerks' to be less stressed and live better.

It is thus very important to develop emotional skills to conquer your vulnerability to situations which can eat you up. Let us see how:

Emotional intelligence in the workplace:

Emotional intelligence in the workplace has four major components:

- Self-awareness – The ability to recognise your emotions and their impact while using gut feelings to guide your decisions.
- Self-management – The ability to control your emotions and behaviour and adapt to changing circumstances.
- Social awareness – The ability to sense, understand and react to other's emotions and feel comfortable socially.
- Relationship management – The ability to inspire, influence and connect to others and manage conflict.

The five key skills of emotional intelligence

There are five key skills that you need to master in order to raise your emotional intelligence and manage stress at work.

- Realise when you're stressed –The best way to reduce stress quickly is through the senses: through sight, sound, smell, taste, and touch. But each person responds differently to sensory input, so you need to find things that soothes and energizes you.

- Stay connected to your internal emotional experience – Your moment-to-moment emotions influence your thoughts and actions, so pay attention to your feelings and factor them into your decision-making at work. If you ignore your emotions you won't be able to fully understand your own motivations and needs, or to communicate effectively with others.

- Recognize and effectively use the nonverbal cues – These make up 95-98% of our communication process. In many cases, what we say is less important than how we say it or the other non-verbal signals we send out, such as eye contact, facial expression, tone of voice, posture, gesture and touch. You also need to be able to accurately read and respond to the non-verbal cues that other people send you at work.

- Develop the capacity to meet challenges with humour– There is no better stress buster than a hearty laugh and nothing reduces stress quicker in the workplace than mutually shared humour. But, if the laugh is at someone else's expense, you may end up with more rather than less stress.

- Resolve conflict positively. Resolving conflict in healthy, constructive ways can strengthen trust between people and diffuse workplace stress and tension. When handling emotionally-charged situations, stay focused in the present by disregarding old hurts and resentments, connect with your emotions, and hear both the words and the non-verbal cues being used. If a conflict can't be resolved, choose to end the argument, even if you still disagree.

Reduce job stress by breaking bad habits

As you learn to manage your job stress and improve your work relationships, you'll have more control over your ability to think clearly and act appropriately. You will be able to break habits that add to your stress at work – and you'll even be able to change negative ways of thinking about things that only add to your stress.

- Eliminate self-defeating behaviour – Many of us make job stress worse with negative thoughts and behaviour. If you can turn around these self-defeating habits, you'll find employer-imposed stress easier to handle.
- Resist perfectionism – No project, situation, or decision is ever perfect, so trying to attain perfection on everything will simply add unnecessary stress to your day. When you set unrealistic goals for yourself or try to do too much, you're setting yourself up to

fall short. Aim to do your best, no one can ask for more than that.

- Clean up your act – If you're always running late, set your clocks and watches fast and give yourself extra time. If your desk is a mess, file and throw away the clutter; just knowing where everything is saves time and cuts stress. Make to-do lists and cross off items as you accomplish them. Plan your day and stick to the schedule – you'll feel less overwhelmed.
- Flip your negative thinking – If you see the downside of every situation and interaction, you'll find yourself drained of energy and motivation. Try to think positively about your work, avoid negative-thinking co-workers, and pat yourself on the back about small accomplishments, even if no one else does.
- Don't try to control the uncontrollable – Many things at work are beyond our control – particularly the behaviour of other people. Rather than stressing out over them, focus on the things you can control such as the way you choose to react to problems.

Five Ways to Dispel Stress

Take time away

When stress is mounting at work, try to take a quick break and move away from the stressful situation. Take a stroll outside the workplace if possible, or spend a few minutes meditating in the break room. Physical movement or finding a quiet place to regain your balance can quickly reduce stress.

- Talk it over with someone. In some situations, simply sharing your thoughts and feelings with someone you trust can help reduce stress. Talking over a problem with someone who is both supportive and empathetic can be a great way to let off steam and relieve stress.
- Connect with others at work. Developing friendship with some of your co-workers can help buffer you from the negative effects of stress. Remember to listen to them and offer support when they are in need as well.
- Look for humour in the situation. When used appropriately, humour is a great way to diffuse stress in the workplace. When you or those around you start taking things too seriously, find a way to lighten the mood by sharing a joke or funny story but it should not be on someone else's expense as it may create more tensions rather than relieving it.

Advertisements Which Misguide The Youth:

I came across an advertisement of a leading Institute, which was trying to lure the youth by its huge lettered advertisement "WE HAVE A HABIT OF WINNING"

– SHAMEFUL! This is what I can say. If everyone wins then who loses? If they have all winners then how do they know anyone is losing? Students of other Institutes maybe ... These institutes are mostly for college drop outs or those preparing for different Entrance Exams. These Institutes by fake counseling, fake data, fake smiles, loot money from the dreaming youth and make their ever-growing fat purse fatter! I do not want to advice against taking coaching or professional certificates but ALWAYS KNOW THAT SOME LOSE AND SOME WIN – LIFE IS A GAME – PLAY YOUR MOVES DEFTLY – IF YOU LOSE ONCE, YOU HAVE TO TRY AGAIN BUT AFTER SEVERAL REPEATED EFFORTS YOU STILL ARE NOT ABLE TO MAKE THEN PROBABLY YOU ARE NOT CUT OUT FOR THAT PROJECT – turn your mind to something else. It is never too late. We have only one life and we have to see that we do not let it go waste! Winning and losing are part of the game called life!

[CHAPTER THREE]

MIND RAPE:

MIND GAME UNFOLDED EMOTIONS!

In the body

Emotion is self-indulgence.

In the vital

Emotion is self-temptation.

In the mind

Emotion is self-mortification.

In the heart

Emotion is self-expansion.

– Sri Chinmoy

"You slut, you bitch. What do you think of yourself?" Prem snarled at his wife and hurling insinuations, pushed her like an unwanted object, for accidentally putting a little more salt in the curry which she cooked for him. This act of his, in no way can be termed a human's behaviour, leave aside a gentleman's! However, the same Prem had different schedule for the woman who was his WIFE IN BED! AND THE WIFE KNEW THAT DENIAL TO HIS ADVANCES COULD BE EVEN MORE FATAL, SO RAPED MENTALLY, SHE ADHERED TO HIS THREATS!

"I know what is on your mind?" The teacher stated sternly to his pupil.

"What?" the pupil asked inquisitively and innocently.

"It is your birthday today, isn't it? But, unless you finish writing the lines hundred times, which I gave you as punishment, arrange the classroom cupboards, clean the window sills, you are not going home to celebrate it! Is that clear," stated the pedagogue.

AN UNKNOWN SPASM OF FEAR CROSSED THE CHILD'S HONEST FACE WHICH WAS BY NOW DRENCHED IN SWEAT.

An IIT student committed suicide because she was continuously ragged by her teacher. Though she had made it to such a prestigious institute, she couldn't manage to pass in one subject due to 'MIND RAPE

GAME'. This 'Mind Rape' syndrome played havoc and she ended her life.

THE ABOVE INSTANCES AND MANY OTHERS OF SUCH KIND ARE NOT INSTANCES OF 'MIND GAME' OR 'CONTROLLING THE MIND' BUT ARE INSTANCES OF 'MIND RAPE OR RAPING THE MIND'.

Emotions are the foundation on which we build lives. They inspire, they limit us. Joy, bliss and happiness along with anger, fear, confusion and unworthiness make us a whole person. BUT SOMETIMES THESE EMOTIONS ARE RAPED SO AS IN A WHOLE THE MINDS ARE RAPED DEFORMING OUR PERSONALITIES AND DOOMING OUR LIVES FOREVER!

According to the Urban Dictionary, Mind rape is when the speaker treats the thoughts of another as if s/he had the ability to intrude into that arena of privacy and the privilege of interpretation as to those thoughts and intentions with respect to them. When a "judge" assigns validity to what is called "circumstantial evidence" in order to reach a conclusion as to the intents and purposes of the "person sought to be charged" for his services as the "accused" of intangible wrong doing.

Not only in India but in almost all countries, in all eras this ancient technique of terrorism and turmoil has played havoc in every field. More than PHYSICAL RAPE, MENTAL RAPE AGONISES AS WE DO NOT KNOW ITS OUTCOME!

The British ruled for about 300 years over countries thousand kilometers away from theirs by following the said technique where the victims were terrorised out of their wits so they were unable to fend for themselves and fed on shit!

In the modern era too such instances are very common and in a way accepted norm at work places. Showing open gestures of lurid lusts, filthy, pervert, objectionable jokes and talks have become a "daily basis affair" in the offices. Indian History's leading lady "Draupadi" is a fine example of this act.

A law has been passed by the Indian Government to protect women from such atrocities at work places, but sadly women working at homes and at other small concerns is not protected by it! AND HOW MANY SUFFERING REALLY KNOCK THE DOORS OF THE POLICE STATIONS OR COURTS? The ladies know the vicious circle of the police system and avoid the unnecessary hassles which ultimately in any society after all malign their names only!

We don't know from when this mind game started but it definitely has made people to part with their self-esteem, respect and valuable personality at times. In dire cases I MYSELF HAVE SEEN PEOPLE CRASHING, LOSING EVEN THEIR VOICE – THEIR FEELINGS and I don't know till when it will go on, but it is said for ages woman have borne the burden of it and it will take ages for it to be wiped out from the face of HUMANITY!

Winning Tricks:

I want all the victims of such games to be patient and walk truly on the path they feel is correct. Listening to inner voice is the best remedy.

To commit suicide or take refuge with drugs is no solution. If someone is maligning you, then the best possible solution is to talk to that bully in front of many.

Do not worry about the result because the event will hardly effect the public; even if it does, it will be short-lived. As it is, even if you do not talk then too you are suffering so it is better to take the risk or chance to come out of the muck. But if it doesn't help then find ways to come out of the environment in which you are dwelling.

MIND RAPE IS A VERY COMMON, EASY AND CHEAP TECHNIQUE USED BY BULLIES TO OVERPOWER THOSE WHO ARE THEIR COMPETITORS. So those suffering must realise that it is the other way round, i.e., the bullies are insecure and in a way suffering! But still I would advise to talk to your friends, well-wishers as sharing really alleviates spirit. Have Courage; Face the world – Win – You have nothing to lose!

[CHAPTER FOUR]

MOST COMMON ABUSE:

EMOTIONAL ABUSE

"Emotional abuse is the most common form of abuse – and yet least talked about. Part of the reason – It is easy for people to overlook is that so that much of what is considered normal and acceptable forms of communication is in fact abusive".

– Kali Munro

Abuse is any kind of behaviour that is knowingly designed to suppress, subjugate and gain undue control over other humans through the use of fear, insinuation, humiliation, guilt, intimidation, coercion, manipulation and many other such gloomy factors.

Emotional Abuse is a kind of abuse which plays mind game on the target or the object. It is not at all physical in nature. Its arena is vast – it can include anything from verbal abuse, constant criticism to such tactics as repeated disapproval or even the refusal to ever be pleased.

Constant berating and belittling under the guise of 'teaching', 'counseling', 'advice', or any other such similar concepts can tarnish and wither the confidence of a person to such an extent as to requiring psychological treatments. It systematically wears out the victim's self-confidence, sense of self-esteem, sense of worthiness and trust in their own perceptions.

Emotional abuse reaches to the very core of the person and gifts with such SCARS which sometimes can't even be wiped out with time's healing process. It is more grievous and serious than physical ones because it slowly eats away the victim's self-esteem and she becomes so beaten down emotionally that instead of getting out of the trap of mind game, she clings to the abuser.

Such victims become so convinced that they are worthless, hence either they end their lives or stay in such abusive situations as they think, they have nowhere to go. In fact the entire social set-up is to be in a way blamed for such happenings.

Winning Trick:

WE ARE THE MENTOR OF OUR LIVES AND WE SHOULD NOT LET NEGATIVE FACTORS DAMPEN OUR SPIRITS. POSITIVE AND NEGATIVE FACTORS BOTH WALK HAND IN HAND. SO INSTEAD

OF CLINGING TO THE ABUSER AND WASTING ENERGY THINKING AND CRYING, WE SHOULD TRY TO COME OUT OF THE TRAP WOVEN FOR US.

IT TAKES TIME – THE ROAD CAN BE BROKEN AND LONG BUT CERTAINLY CAN BE ATTAINED AND MENDED IF WE HAVE THE WILL POWER. EVEN IF WE DON'T, WE CAN CULTIVATE!

Look at the positivity in your life. Life itself is a positive happening. Fear of walking out of any relationship, is frightening – you feel you'll be laughed at but have you thought seriously, HOW MANY OF US HAVE REMEMBERED ANY PERSON'S TRAUMA FOR LONG?

Emotional Abuse is not only directed towards women. I know many men who suffer abuse at the hands of women. Youth are also trapped in this net of emotional abuse. Realise that you are being abused – talk with your near ones and find ways to over come it. No use bearing it and wasting years of your precious life on it.

Winning Secret:

Look at those who are your ideals or whom you idolise. Are they without any lacuna? See any actor, player, and writer, celebrity or your near and dear ones. Didn't they have bad patches or some ill-doings attached to them, but still you idolise them!

Your family, when growing up, taught you how to walk, how to speak, or how to drive a car. These are basic skills that you LEARNED when you needed them. You have also learned from your family this helpless attitude, this automatic acceptance of 'power attitudes' used by abusers in the name of PERSEVERANCE. Now you need to drop them and find other skills that are going to boost your self-esteem and make you stop accepting and begin to reject this emotional abuse.

So Life is the way we perceive, not the way others force us to perceive. People's memory is bad – Make Best Use of It and Live Your Life – Don't Let It Long – Win it!

[CHAPTER FIVE]

PANGS OF PERSEVERANCE:

IS IT JUSTIFIED?

Perseverance according to Lexicon means the act of persevering; persistence in anything undertaken; continued pursuit or prosecution of any business, or enterprise begun. Holding onto anything or something until your dream is achieved. HOLDING ONTO ANYTHING TILL WE SUCCEED!!!

Many would like to disagree with it BUT STILL there are many who believe. As I have said earlier too – to believe or not to believe in anything is a person's personal choice but certainly people who have walked on thorny paths can guide and warn others.

Perseverance is always thought to have A POSITIVE MEANING ATTACHED TO IT. BUT I DO NOT FULLY AGREE WITH IT. It can have a positive shade attached to it if you want to achieve something rather tough, fruitful in life but what if one wants to hold onto such dreams which never has any meaning or positivity attached to it. Like wanting to marry a particular girl or to start a business which is beyond one's reach! I am not discouraging anyone.

TO DREAM BIG IS GOOD BUT TO BE PRACTICAL IS EVEN BETTER. Now again this practicality should not be mistaken to be "synonymous of being emotionless". We have to be emotional in our relationships but sometimes to maintain one relation we have to sacrifice the other. Now it is up to us to think which relationship or liaison is good for us and the society as a whole.

Someone has quoted:

> "I was early taught to work as well as play,
> My life has been one long, happy holiday;
> Full of work and full of play —
> I dropped the worry on the way —
> And God was good to me every day."

BUT IT SEEMS THE WRITER HAS VIEWED ONLY ONE SIDE OF PERSEVERANCE – If delved deeply into the meaning of it, we can see and realise many aspects attached to this wonderful quote. Here the speaker had "an understanding guide". He only had to work and play; hence his life was more like a holiday as he patiently listened to his guide and adhered to it.

But how many of us are as accurately lucky as "the quote above"? Is patiently relenting to the tortures inflicted on us being termed as perseverance? Last year, I WAS TRAUMATISED BY THE BEHAVIOUR OF THE PASSPORT OFFICE IN DELHI. Despite, everything rightly done, the passport of my son had a mistake in the address and I had to run twice to the office as he himself was busy with his internship. Now do you think perseverance in such cases is correct? Don't you think it is

high time we do away with such perseverance and VOICE OUR RIGHTS AGAINST SUCH NEGLIGENCE?

So we see that perseverance always is not good and commendable! Like many women of our country suffer incessantly and die "dowry deaths" because from their very childhood they have been taught to be "patient" and show "perseverance".

However it does have positive effects too. For instance to achieve anything in life, "no short-cuts" are advised. A short-cut road is mostly seen to be hazardous, hence to achieve anything in life WE HAVE TO HOLD ON TO OUR DREAMS BUT SHOULD NOT MAKE IT AN OBSESSION, as when not achieved many resort to behavioural extremes like doing drugs, alcohol, etc thereby dooming their lives.

A Winner's Guide:

So if after all the perseverance, you do not get what you wanted in life don't let yourself drowned in the ocean of negativity and shut your lives in catacombs because your life is not only yours – there are many people who love you and are attached to you.

THERE IS NOTHING WRONG IN DREAMING BIG BUT IF AT ALL THE DREAM DOES NOT TURN INTO REALITY, JUST OVERLOOK IT AS "A DREAM" AND START AFRESH. IT IS NEVER-EVER LATE!

[CHAPTER SIX]

PEER PRESSURE:

DO NOT LET YOUR MIND BE TAMED: BE YOUR OWN MASTER

"I want the same doll as Clara's, Sara whimpered and cried the whole day till her parents didn't give in to her demand. Rosaline, Sara's mother was totally confused with her three-year-olds' ever increasing demand. Actually she failed to understand what a psychiatrist would have understood, i.e. Sara, even at a tender age of three had become a victim of the 'PEER PRESSURE SYNDROME'!

Peer Pressure refers to the influence exerted by a PEER GROUP in encouraging a person to change his or her ATTITUDES, VALUES, or BEHAVIOUR in order to

CONFORM to group NORMS. Social groups affected include membership groups, when the individual is "formally" a member for example, political party, trade union, or a social clique.

A person affected by peer pressure may or may not want to belong to these groups. They may also recognise dissociative groups with which they would not wish to associate, and thus they behave adversely concerning that group's behaviours.

Peer pressure can cause people to do things they would not normally do, e.g. promote hatred, take drugs, smoke, get a girlfriend, marry, get a job, have children, buy items they don't really need (cars, houses, boats), etc. This is the dictionary meaning of it.

Peer pressure at times can be killing and it is not that only children of High Schools AND Colleges are undergoing or rather suffering it. Even a three-year-old Sarah wants a doll same as her friend because her "Status" needs "A BOOST".

The level of peer influence generally increases in the growing years of children, and resistance to peer influence often declines as children gain independence from the family or caregivers, and before they fully form an adult identity. Pre-school children tend to be the least aware of peer pressure, and are the least influenced by the need to conform. However with more social interactions outside the home and more awareness of others, the influence of peers increases.

Students in colleges these days not only cope up with studies but they also have to look "handsome", "macho" and so on ... the list is never ending. Sometimes trivial matters like "teasing" or "taunting" which is another form of bullying takes lives of children – either the "silent one ends up his life" or "unbelievable but true takes the life of those bullying him"!

The consequences sometimes are dangerous and parents, teachers, well-wishers have to take actions within time. The ever increasing suicidal rates are alarming making people to sit up and think where exactly things are going wrong?

Winning Trick:

Yes guys – Parents and well-wishers are not always there with you. You have to decide what is good for

you. Things which seem so serious become trivial with the passage of time. So do not let petty, unwanted happenings taint your life and personality forever.

Before it is too late the society as a whole has to come forward as a help or else every day we are reading serious articles on this ever growing issue! We are all well aware of this but still presume that situation will come under control on its own – we can close our eyes to what is happening in the name of ragging and easing pressure of exams, losing girlfriends, etc. Students resort to uncalled means, like drugs, alcohol, smoking, petty thievery to maintain their lifestyle.

Who will help such dejected elements? Surely we have to do so – if required medication; counseling and means to bring them back to the mainstream should be adopted. SO GET UP AND BE A HELP BEFORE IT IS TOO LATE!

I would request those who are unnecessarily facing this syndrome to be their own helpers as no one is going to help them. DON'T GET HYPNOTISED. The things which seem so grievous at school/college level hardly has any meaning once you enter the mainstream of life

– There are thousand reasons to crib and millions to be happy. Now it is up to you if you want to ruin this one life or make it fulfilling so when after years you look back, you are able to say, "YES I DID IT".

[CHAPTER SEVEN]

DATING THE RAPE

DO NOT INVITE RAPES WHILE YOU DATE.

SAY "HELLO" TO A NEW YEAR WITH SMILE AND NO REGRETS!

When the year 2010, was silently slipping into its catacomb, a very close friend of mine, a brilliant Engineer, Arti called me, "Rashmi, write something about the year drifting. Only an hour is left..."

Yes the reality, only an hour is left and so many happenings are taking place. I could hear people almost in frenzied revelry prepared to welcome the new year, with blasting music – their celebration non-ending, not even realising what exactly are they celebrating!

Another friend who had just escaped a scene from one of the most renowned shopping mall of Noida, rang me up and was hysterical...she could not control her sobs and recounted, as how she managed to escape the fangs of lechers but her other friends were still being ruthlessly molested among the silent spectators with the police nowhere in tow for rescue!

All this made me to ponder over P.B.SHELLY'S lines, "the locks of the approaching storm – *thou dirge…of the DYING YEAR, TO WHICH THIS CLOSING NIGHT WILL BE THE DOME OF VAST SEPULCHRE* ... and was he wrong? Every 31st December, aren't we in a way singing DIRGE (FUNERAL SONG) to the "dying year"?

Shelly was perceived as pessimistic but what are those practicing lechery on these nights? Are they being optimistic? They do not spare even their friends and using them for their benefits they pounce upon them deceitfully......AND SURELY THE NIGHT INSTEAD OF BRINGING HAPPINESS IS BRINGING MENTAL DEATH FOR MANY...THE GRIEVOUS MATTER OF CONCERN– WHAT IS RESPONSIBLE TO THE DEATH OF EVERY LAST NIGHT OF ANY YEAR? ISN'T IT TO SOME EXTENT "DATE RAPES WHERE THE GIRLS THEMSELVES ARE DATING RAPES! THE BOYS WHO CAN NOT WIN OVER A CERTAIN GIRL TRY IT WITH SEDATIVES!

AND I CAN TOO LIKE SHELLY, PERCEIVE LOCKS OF THE APPROACHING STORM – READY TO ENGULF HUMANITY!

According to Wikipedia, Date Rape, is often referred to as "acquaintance rape", is an assault usually committed by a new acquaintance, involving sexual intercourse without mutual consent!

Friends Or Strangers?

Mostly or we can say very commonly it happens among the friends and sometimes strangers too, when girls meet online and date. The current trend of meeting online and dating has added more headaches for the police.

But sometimes known friends too mix drugs in the drinks of their friends which is odourless and has dire effects... so much so that, usually after the party is over and finally when the girl comes to her senses, she is not able to decide whether she has been raped or not!

These drugs can sometimes lead to brutal mass or gang rape and even death for many! So a minute of enjoyment for the accuser becomes oceans of sorrow for the parents of the victim as well as the victimizer.

Date Drug:

The most common drug is Rohypnol which is not approved for use in the US and its importation is banned. Illicit use of Rohypnol began in Europe in the 1970's and started appearing in the US in the early 1990's, where it became to be known as "rophies" "roofies" "roach", "rope" ...and so a DATE DRUG WAS BORN!

Counseling at all level should not only be given to the girls but boys should also be instructed in a similar manner. THEY CAN RUIN THEIR CAREER JUST FOR A MOMENT OF SILLY JOY. So that we can do away with this adage that ONE HAS TO PAY THE PRICE OF PROGRESS.

Warning and Winning Tricks:

STRICT ADVICE TO THE GIRLS:

1. Never let anyone buy you a drink – however this can be a morale booster but strictly avoid it.

2. Never let anyone carry your drink to you.
3. Don't leave your glass unattended.
4. Always carry your cell phone with yourself and don't let others use it.
5. Dial your Parents', Police, or any other relatives' number and save it in call register so that in case of any emergency you can just redial.
6. Most importantly your program i.e. dates time venue, etc should be prefixed and should not change.
7. In case of any change inform your friends and relatives.
8. AND ABOVE ALL IF POSSIBLE ABSTAIN FROM ALCOHOL OR AT LEAST TRY RETURNING HOME WITHIN THE SCHEDULED TIME.

So celebrate as much you want....Dance as much you want...

BECKON NEW YEAR...BECKON VALENTINE'S DAY... BECKON WHATEVER YOU WANT BUT ALWAYS REMEMBER SOMEONE IS WATCHING YOU...READY TO TAKE YOUR ADVANTAGE. SO IT'S BETTER TO BE SAFE THAN SORRY!

[CHAPTER EIGHT]

NUDITY

A MIND SUDOKO

Long back, nudity was used as a weapon to lay Saints astray and deviate them from their path of meditation. Like the Indian saint Vishwamitra whose "tapasya" or deep meditation was disrupted by the intoxicating beauty of the apsara, Menaka!

But the present generation feels if the saints "had gone astray – it was because their minds saw "nudity in beauty"! But if they would have thought there was no wrong in their acts, then they could have boldly and positively faced everything coming in their strides. The Gen Y or the Internet Generation certainly opines differently from Gen X !

Some philosophers too think NUDITY IS IN THE MIND OF PEOPLE. According to such philosophers we, "need to open our minds to view the world and its inhabitants in their natural state. No other animal is ashamed to show off their bodies...it is humankind who has perversed the course of nature by creating a false aura around the human body. On a warm day, or in warm countries, it would be perfectly natural and would be considered to be common sense to remain naked."

BUT IS IT REALLY SO? IS NUDITY A STATE OF MIND? If it is really a state of mind then shouldn't we all do away with keeping ourselves clad and going nude at public places. Now I think such philosophers dwell in a state of UTOPIA! We cannot run away from this fact that NUDITY ATTRACTS—SEX SELLS!

Pick up any newspaper or surf any channel on the television. Half of the advertisements are displaying semi-nude or sometimes fully nude pictures and clips of women selling items which have no relevance "of their beautiful bodies" with the products.

Whether it is cement, milk products, hair brushes, hair dryers, computers, furniture, cell phones, cars, trucks, buses, air conditioners, fans, jewellery, almost any and everything has an attachment "of a woman's luscious body" – now what does this signify? It is very-very simple. If NUDITY IS A STATE OF MIND THEN IT IS HIGH TIME WE SHOULD DO AWAY WITH THIS STATE. THEN WHY ARE WE SELLING THINGS EXCITING THE MINDS OF COMMON PEOPLE?

Winning Tricks:

NUDITY AT COLLEGE/SCHOOL/WORKPLACE NOT RECOMMENDED:

To gain instant popularity, the current generation very easily clings on to nudity while dressing-up for college/ school/workplace. The thought behind is to get fast fame like 2 minutes noodles. Clothes worn at any such place should be comfortable and not provocative. Provocative clothes like fast foods can be dangerous to health and your future. In fact, instead of attracting, it carries a bad message to the bosses or your peers. Girls can attract lechers and workplace bosses can look at them as 'easily available material'. The girls should realise 'they are not material'; they are at par with men and should be treated with respect.

Clothesandaccessorieswornshouldenhance,andbeautify your personality. They can be simple, clean, ironed and well-kept. Bought from the local market or branded stores, they really should do justice to your looks.

Abstain from nudity at such places as you are not going to win anything out of it.

The Truth – To View Nudity in All Its Beauty is Encouraged.

(But this viewpoint is for Philosophers and Poets)

It is high time we realise that we cannot do away with this state – it exists and will exist exciting the entire human clan for ages to come. I think it is useless gibbering over an aspect which has existed since Adam's time and if it had not existed THE PRESENT HUMAN RACE ON THIS PLANET WOULD HAVE NOT COME INTO EXISTENCE. So one thing is crystal clear – the fragrance of nudity has intoxicated even the geniuses of the poets. BUT THIS DOESN'T MEAN I ADVOCATE IT – I AM SIMPLY MAKING YOU REALISE, NUDITY IS BEAUTIFUL WHEN PRESENTED AESTHETICALLY AT THE RIGHT PLACE, WITH RIGHT ACUMEN AND IN THE RIGHT ENVIORNMENT! FOR EXAMPLE, YOU CAN SLEEP IN THE BED NUDE BUT YOU CAN'T WALK TO YOUR WORKPLACE IN THE SAME WAY. I know at times, the concept of nudity can prove to be a MIND SUDOKO but Man is a social animal and if we have to live in the society then it is our duty to see that we do not provoke the sleeping animal lurking silently around every man's mind…

Let us read the lines below and give our frantic minds some soothing tranquiliser.

"Of naked stone, with a lot of arousal left behind,
Almost like flesh, only cold instead,
Even though our hands are penniless and empty,
They are filled with man's destiny to love and be loved,
So similar to the divine in repose, we lay upon rose
Petals in our scalloped shells nibbling on poppies,
Reading poetry and singing songs of naked love."

– Joyce White.

[CHAPTER NINE]

BED BUDDIES

OR FRIENDS WITH BENEFITS (FWB) IS IT REALLY THE UNVIELED TRUTH!

The New Genre Columns! Give More Wrapped Titillation – Earn More Money!

Overworked, totally drained and collapsing on bed, my eyes were searching to read something light and interesting – no heavy news – no devastating details – no geniuses junk...only something which could ease, relax my taut, tortured mind and body! I reached out for the weekly edition of Tuesday, 7th December, 2010, lying near my bed carelessly. Probably someone had taken it out to wrap some item. Flipping randomly through its pages my eyes stationed at a column, "BED BUDDIES OR FRIENDS WITH BENEFIT", in its variety section.

Now this certainly was something which at once hypnotised me with its magnetic magnitude provocation of words and concocted incidents (as I feel there were no real life examples quoted, except that the writer was forcing her opinion and titillating common minds) with two skimpy interviews AND was certainly successful in drawing roving eyes. At least I believe this because she did get a reader in me and likewise might have got many others too!

Actually the writer herself was totally confused with this "research" of hers as she like a medical practitioner was advocating, Friends with Benefits' and that it was not a bad way to go about. BUT THEN AT THE END SHE SAYS THIS TOO – THAT FWB IS NOT THAT EASY. SHE THEN SUGGESTS CERTAIN DOS AND DON'TS! Phew!!

THE WRITER MUST BE CONGRATULATED FOR THIS CONCEPT OF HERS! AND HIGHLIGHTING THE ABBREVIATION FOR IT (FWB, which no doubt exists).

Where parents and society is striving hard to attain and achieve the lost morality in the "young generation" or why only the young – the more mature ones too, PEOPLE ARE COMING UP WITH INNOVATIVE IDEAS OF SEXUAL RELATIONSHIPS! ALL APPLAUD TO COLUMNISTS WHO INSTEAD OF TAKING THE

SOCIETY ON AN HONEST PATH IS HIGHLIGHTING WAYS FOR SEXUAL INNOVATIONS!

Now if someone is a "friend" how can that relationship be of "benefit". Little or less but it does involve emotions and friends if jump into bed accidentally or knowingly cannot have a "benefit" factor!

"BEDDING FOR BUSINESSES" is something which was always there and it is our moral duty to guide the current generation – make them realise what is wrong and what is right AND NOT CONFUSE THEM WITH A FASHIONABLE TERM LIKE 'BED BUDDIES'! (Now business gratification can be sexual to gain some important assignment, involving no emotions).

Even, if at a time one is seeing two people, he/she is surely to lose one relationship and I mean "relationship" – A BUSINESS DEALING IS ENTIRELY DIFFERENT – BUSINESS PARTNERS CAN NOT BE "BUDDIES"! I too have like others, exercised my "freedom of speech and expression" and in no way will I misguide anyone and a make a beautiful experience, "a matter of fact".

Good that at least she has suggested the people doing sex in such liaisons to be careful and carry condoms – so again she goes haywire – it seems people are always looking forward to such encounters everyday! However in the end she has said that maintaining "FWB" can be troublesome and has asked ones ENTERING INTO

IT TO STICK TO GROUND RULES. Now this expert should be asked WHAT ARE GROUND RULES? Can a heart be tutored not to love anybody after having sex?

Now going through another article of another Weekly there was another similar read targeted to titillate senses – actually it seems the "variety section" is always flavoured up with SEX SPICE AND EVEN IF THEY ARE BADLY SCROUNGING, CAN NOT FIND ANY OTHER AROMA! GOOD they are coming up with tabooed topic like "KAMASUTRA", etc. but we all know that excess of any diet causes indigestion!

AND THIS IS MY WARNING TO THE YOUTH. SEX IS NOT BAD BUT YOU SHOULD BE AWARE OF ITS CONSEQUENCES AND LIABILITIES. You have to earn it, just as you earn your bread! Eating outside can be harmful, so a casual fling can end into a sexual trap ruining your mental health. To have sex for the sake of having and forgetting will make us animals!

Warning and Winning Trick:

NEVER MIX FRIENDS AND FRIENDSHIP WITH BENEFIT OR BUSINESS.

I know it's your life and ultimately you have to lead it not I. Sex is an enjoyable experience and a relished topic, no doubt but I REQUEST YOU NOT TO MAKE IT MECHANICAL – The more mechanical it becomes, the more materialistic the world gets – and more likely you can find yourself depressed and down.

Emotions are the pillars on which we build our personalities and entire life. SO HAVE A PINCH OF EMOTION IN EVERY SEX ENCOUNTER – BE IT WITH YOUR FRIENDS OR BUDDIES – IT MAY NOT LEAD TO A PERMANENT RELATIONSHIP BUT DEFINITELY IT WILL NOT BE A BURDEN ON YOUR SOUL AND MIND.

I know the present generation very quickly adapts itself to the ongoing trend of moving away from one relationship to another but THERE ARE STILL MANY WHO FIND IT DIFFICULT TO COME OUT OF "THE BED BUDDIES SITUATION"! So once again I ask my readers to think and enter in any kind of such situations even for business gratification as physical relationship can be of minutes but its music can be heard even long after the actual act!

Winner's Guide:

HERE ARE SOME DIRE CONSEQUENCES OF THIS CONCEPT, (TAKEN FROM DECCAN HERALD)

"But isn't there a risk factor attached to such relationships?" Explains Dr Prashanth Soundarajan, a consultant sexologist with a popular city hospital, "The biggest risk is that of contracting sexually transmitted disease (STDs). Several youngsters approach me on a daily basis with problems and queries concerning casual sex. Even if you trust your friend with your life, it's always advisable to use some form of protection to avoid problems in the future."

Agreeing with him is Deepa Abraham, a psychologist and counselor, "Previously having an intimate relationship such as this, only happened post-marriage. But things have changed a lot since a few years and havoc with the various relationships they have around them. Having casual affairs don't raise too many eyebrows. However in this case, such people run the risk of turning sex-addicts. If their emotions are not kept under check it could lead to a lot of complications and even create serious problems leading to deaths!

So a simple question, I would like to ask – Is life given to you to ruin over matters which later in your life may seem trivial! I understand, sex is a physical need which cannot be avoided or overlooked. But then don't most of the things in our lives hold the same importance. Don't your parents advise to limit your expenses! Doesn't your wife ask to check your alcohol consumption, similarly

SEX TOO SHOULD BE INVESTED THOUGHTFULLY AND EMOTIONALLY!

However, I do not also suggest to be over emotional to any relationship so, that you abstain from getting hyper when it breaks BUT, I WANT PEOPLE NOT TO MEDDLE CASUAL SEX WITH FRIENDSHIP IN ANY CASE.

So we see, EMOTION IS THE MAIN AND BASIC INGREDIENT OF BEING A HUMAN! This one ingredient segregates us from animals – saves us from being inhumane and makes us worth staying on this planet.

Success and progress doesn't mean that we have to deal 'Sex' factor mechanically. C'mon guys, lead a NORMAL LIFE – Enter any relationship when you are ready, feel for it and have the most important ingredient for such relationships – EMOTIONS! If the opposite sex wants to have a casual relationship with you, don't perceive it as a golden chance because later on it can create problems if one of you feel that 'Emotion' is troubling you! Sex is not wrong but it should be respected!

[CHAPTER TEN]

KILL THE GLOBAL KILLER

BEFORE IT KILLS YOU

"Anger Says:
I Can Destroy
The Whole World"
Peace Says:
"Not When I Work
Inside You".

– *Sri Chinmoy*

- Almost two years ago, a sixteen-year-old boy, brutally butchered his classmate, because he was constantly bullied by him. The offender, considered to be otherwise very shy, could not take the torturous tirade anymore. As both his parents were busy with their professional lives, he decided to end "this traumatic situation", on his own!

- In a gruesome incident, a twenty-year-old boy killed his very own mother because he was denied access to the "lone computer in their house" as he was addicted to porn sites!
- Almost everyday, villages of Haryana (India), witness heinous incidents of "Honour Killings" where couples are given death punishments for marrying in the same "gotra"(subcaste). Who can say, that we are, still not living in the "Barbaric Age" or why are we denying this fact that our villages too have "Talibani" kind of rule!
- It is believed; a father killed his own teenage daughter, in New Delhi, when he caught her in a lucid sexual act with her servant!
- A man in a rage of fury, spat at his boss in his office and lost his job which supported his family of five...
- In a heart rending incident, a doctor from Gurgaon, India was brutally beaten to death, over a petty issue of "parking space" by two drunkard youths.
- And who can forget the MANY TERRORIST ACTIVITIES CLAIMING LIVES GLOBALLY!
- The Iraq war has forever marred the face of humanity by excessive show of anger in the form of heinous rapes, murder and brutal torture.

RAGE, ANGER, FURY, and with many more names, this human trait results in devastating activities mentioned above. Even LYSSA, Goddess of Anger, would be ashamed, that why did she ever choose to dominate the field which has become "A KILLER"!

ANGER KNOWS NO LIMITS – IT HAS NO TAMER - OUR SOULS DIRECTING OUR MINDS CAN ONLY TAME AND CHAIN THE WILD SPURT OF FIERY VOLCANO OF OUR EMOTIONS!

The problem with anger, as Aristotle observed over 2,500 years ago, is that – Anyone can become angry – that is easy. But to be angry with the right person, to the right

degree, at the right time, for the right purpose, and in the right way – this is not easy.

Really, this is undoubtedly a great problem. Thinkers and Philosophers guide us to channelise our anger and show it only when it is extremely necessary! But is it possible to do so? No I can never agree to it as anger is a rage of a moment which when unleashed swallows everything which comes in its way! This feeling will not warn you or provide any premonitions to the repercussions it may lead to but will certainly leave behind it, an ocean of Disaster!

In fact we are no saints, when continuous anger sparks are shot at us, it sometimes really becomes too difficult for us to maintain our cool. A very close friend of mine, one day rang me up with uncontrollable tears. According to her, though married for twenty years, she has never known the "love of a husband". From morning to night she is slogging for her family and her husband – a complete moron compared to her, insinuates cunningly only at home as he has projected a very fine image of himself at his workplace! Now when things went beyond her control, she too has started shouting at him, using abusive language!

HER PAIN AND PERSEVERANCE WAS NOT READY TO MAKE PEACE WITH HER INNER SELF.

So we see to let peace work is not so easy – There is a great difference in PREACHING AND PRACTISING.

But still I am going to put forth some points to channelise your mind and soul in MOMENTS OF RAGE! Let us analyse a few points:

1. Are you often angry?
2. Do you frequently overreact?
3. Do you take your anger out on someone other than the person you are angry with?
4. Do you hold grudges, sulk?
5. Do you dwell in a state of anger for a long time?
6. Are you scared of your anger?
7. Does your anger spoil your work and relationships?
8. AND THE MOST IMPORTANT – DO YOU GET VIOLENT AND EXHIBIT THIS VIOLENCE WHEN ANGRY?

If you answered yes to two or more of these questions, you may have a problem dealing with anger. And anger may be keeping you from communicating effectively.

Hence we see Anger as one of the most important and complex feeling in the range of human emotions which causes a great deal of suffering! And when one drowns in this ocean of disaster it is difficult to surface a new life.

Hence a simple advise – if it is not easy to let go things, forgive and forget – think after your rage, outbursts – what harm will it cost to people close to you!

Winning Guide:

Apart from YOGA and MEDITATION, adopting any kind of hobby like swimming, reading, writing, in fact penning down your feelings making your anger and loss constructive rather destructive. Painting, cooking, knitting playing outdoor games or even loitering uselessly around with friends can even help to control this KILLER WHICH HAS TAKEN A GLOBAL FORM SWALLOWING HUMANITY.

NOT FOR YOURSELF BUT FOR THE PEOPLE YOU CARE, PLEASE BE AWARE OF YOUR NEGATIVE ATTITUDES! IF YOU CANNOT DO SO YOU MAY EVEN CONSULT A PSYCHIATRIST – THERE IS NO SHAME IN IT. AFTER ALL WE ARE HUMANS WITH COMMON FOLLIES AND NOT GODS.

[CHAPTER ELEVEN]

HOW TO MANAGE ANGER

Anger is one of the most primal and complex feelings in the range of human emotions. Although it is neither good nor bad, its misuse causes a great deal of suffering:

- Undermining trust, loyalty, and teamwork.
- Destroying relationships.
- Creating a hostile environment.
- Lowering productivity.
- Contributing to health problems.
- Incurring legal expenses.
- Contributing to violence.

ANGER CAN BE POSITIVE TOO

Anger does three things which in a way can be positive.

1. It alerts us to a problem. It's like a siren, warning us of a threat to our safety or to the safety of those we care for.
2. It focuses our attention. When we're angry, we have trouble thinking about anything else.
3. It gives us energy. Anger floods the bloodstream with chemicals that turbo charge the body and prepare it to take action.

Here's an example of anger in action. A department store floor manager, late for a meeting and thinking about 10 different problems, overhears an associate call a customer a "fat cow". She stops dead in her tracks. For the moment she forgets everything else. She steps in to deal with the customer and the employee.

Since each person's response to anger is unique, you have become an expert about your anger pattern.

How to Channel Your Emotions in a Positive Direction:

Winning Tricks:

A few good channeling techniques may include....

- Removing yourself – Get away from what's causing you to have negative emotions. Do anything to distance yourself from the person or situation making you upset.

- Doing something positive – If you have righteous anger over social issues, don't just have a meltdown but do something constructive. Write a letter to a newspaper editor expressing your opinions; write your congressional representative, etc.
- Getting physical – Take a walk. Go bowling. Shoot basketball hoops. Run. Channel your bad feelings into something that releases endorphins. Neurotransmitters produced in the brain that reduce pain, endorphins can change a negative mood.
- Breathing deeply – First, get comfortable. Then slowly take in deep breaths, breathing in from your abdomen. This helps to still a racing pulse, as well as calm your mind. Check your muscle tension (especially in the shoulders, neck, and jaw). As you relax any tight areas, picture a peaceful scene, centering your thoughts on positive images.
- Talking to someone – Whether it's a trusted friend or professional, you need to talk out your feelings before you can heal. Look for a support group where you feel free to share your deepest emotions. The worst path you can take is to isolate and not reach out for help.
- Journaling – Journaling (writing out your feelings on paper) is an excellent way to manage your emotions.

You don't have to show anyone what you wrote. It's just between yourself and God. Then, after you've released what's bothering you, tear up your paper if you don't need to rehearse it.

Most of all, pray. Talk to God about how you feel. Pour out your heart to him. He knows all about it anyway, but it helps to verbalise your feelings. Faith is that element which helps you overpower all negative situations.

Wait Until Emotions Are Under Control to Address Problem/Situation.

This means that in the workplace, the general situation generated while facing onslaughts of anger:

- Situations, problems, and/or concerns appear worse when you are angry.
- If you speak before getting your anger under control, you may say things that create more problems.
- Negative emotions create tension.
- Taking time to develop a possible solution to your problem before taking action helps you resolve the situation.
- When you wait until emotions are under control to address a problem/situation, you have an essential career soft skill.

Keep Voice Even and Calm When Upset

This means that in the workplace:

- The tone of your voice is important; it may indicate a problem when there is none.
- An angry voice will keep emotions high.
- It has a calming effect when co-workers see you with your anger under control.
- When you keep your voice even and calm when upset, you have an essential career soft skill.

Case Study 1 : A Web Help

Jills' morning did not start well. Her little boy got out of bed with a temperature which meant he could not go to day care. Jill made several phone calls before she found a friend who would stay with her son. Jill looked at the clock. If she hurried, she would only be 10 minutes late for work. As Jill got into the car, the battery was dead because the door had not been closed. She quickly headed to the bus stop without calling her supervisor. The bus arrived 15 minutes late.

When Jill arrived at work, she was over an hour late. She was stressed and angry at the world. Her co-workers were busy. Jill had forgotten the big sale in the store. Customers were waiting for help. Her supervisor was very upset with her lack of responsibility. Jill would need to work late to make up the time she missed.

Jill was angry with herself and totally upset when her boss spoke to her about her being late. She was worried about her sick child and anxious about what it would cost to get a new battery. With each passing hour, Jill's mood got worsened and it showed in her attitude. She took her anger out on her co-workers and customers by snapping at them. Tension increased. Jill felt she was being treated unfairly. Nobody understood her situation.

Case Study 2: That day was the birthday of Rohan's girlfriend's. He had meticulously planned every detail of the party. He wanted to prove it to her that he was indeed the best choice she had ever made in life. But as he got up in the morning, he found his father to be seriously sick with his diabetes and blood pressure crashing. Serious help was needed. Rohan had to take him to the hospital, hoping he would be released soon, but the doctors advised to admit him.

Rohan's mother Laxmi was around but the situation required him to be there the entire day. He once tried to escape by stating some urgent work to the doctors but was snubbed that nothing more was important than his father's life.

He was caught in an ugly middle situation – to choose between his family and girlfriend. His anger started mounting and most of the time in the room, despite his father's critical situation; he was taking it out on his mother. He had with lots of patience won over this girl and now according to him everything was ruined.

He blamed his fate. It was not that he didn't love his family – it was only that he believed he was unlucky forgetting the most important point that if the girl too had seriously loved him, she would be beside him instead of partying out with her other friends!

Winning Trick:

Applying What You Know

From anger proceeds delusion; from delusion confused memory; from confused memory the destruction of reason; from destruction of reason you perish. ...THIS IS WHAT WE SAW EXACTLY HAPPENING IN THE ABOVE CASES!

SO DON'T PERISH – CHANNELISE THE SPURTS POSITIVELY AND BE A WINNER!

[CHAPTER TWELVE]

EFFECTIVE COMMUNICATION

PATH TO SUCCESS

Effective Communication according to me is an important ingredient of success. Some are blessed with this skill by birth but some need to improve on it. Here is an honest post from my side to help those who desire to hone and polish this skill leading to their ever growing success and enhancing their personality.

Effective communication is all about conveying your messages to other people clearly and unambiguously. It's also about receiving information that others are sending to you, with as little distortion as possible.

Doing this involves effort from both the sender of the message as well as the receiver. And it's a process that can be tinted with error, messages improperly delivered by the sender, or misinterpreted by the recipient. When this isn't detected, it can cause tremendous confusion, wasted effort and missed opportunity. Communication is a very powerful instrument and to get across it honestly is extremely important. It can create a negative or positive effect, so it is highly desirable that the message intended for the person is delivered across positively without any distortion.

In fact, communication is only successful when both the sender and the receiver understand the same information as a result of the communication.

By successfully getting your message across, you convey your thoughts and ideas effectively. When not successful, the thoughts and ideas that you actually send do not necessarily reflect what you think, causing a communication breakdown and creating roadblocks that stand in the way of your goals – both personally and professionally.

Communication sometimes is your way of perception of certain things. An extremely wealthy man took his son to the country side to actually perceive what poverty is like. After spending a day and night there with a very poor family, the father thought that his message of "showering wealth on his son and that he is very lucky to have a father like him" must have gone down well with the son but the message which he wanted to communicate was not taken as desired. The son after the visit told his father that the realisation that how poor he was has now dawned upon him after this visit. He realised that "he had only one swimming pool whereas the poor man had a full river to him",.."they had only one dog but the man had four", ... and so on.....So we see here a fine example of "miscommunication".

Winning Tricks:

A person can anytime improve his communication skill if he has a positive attitude towards life and things happening around him. The first prerequisite of developing good communication skill is "developing positive perception towards life".

Many other things too comprise the ingredient of fine communication like:

1. Feeling at ease while communicating.
2. Choice of correct words and phrases.
4. Proper body language i.e. avoiding unnecessary fidgeting of limbs or sending wrong signals.
5. Reading novels, current affairs on internet or in newspapers, watching news. A well-informed person can only interact positively.

6. Eye contact but not actually foolishly staring at the person addressed to.
7. Work on certain paper exercise before any speech execution.
8. No one is perfect, so don't be overburdened with the baggage of "feeling confident".
9. Be your natural self and have confidence + faith in your aptitude and skill.
10. Be open to criticism and take it in – good humour – don't let criticism ruin your confidence. Remember there are always certain people around you who are jealous and want to pull you down.
11. AND THE MOST IMPORTANT ONE IS TO BE A GOOD LISTENER.

Good and effective communication can be your key to success and an ambiguous communication can ruin you. So think twice before you open your mouth. Useless gibbering and angling for appreciation can be dangerous to your career.

Give respect to those who command it and be pleasant to those who don't. Being vicious and unnecessary sycophancy will lead you nowhere.

Keep away from "disparaging words and attitude but at the same time don't be disparaged".

Learn to manage your talent and send across your message pleasantly. Nothing is going to help you except your positive self-esteem, positive perception of things in a given situation and harnessing the various opportunities strewn all around you. So have faith and develop effective communication with your will power.

[CHAPTER THIRTEEN]

SEXUAL MYTHS

A sex myth is a false belief about sexual behaviour or physiology that is either scientifically incorrect or downright apocryphal. Sex myths are misleading and can have negative repercussions on the youth.

There are many common rumours which end up messing up the lives of the youths. This chapter is incorporated to make the youth conscious and aware of their selves and to refrain them from visiting quacks. It is generally seen that they feel ashamed to discuss such topics with their elders who too are wary to guide them. These days we have counsellors in most of the educational institutions but because of the age-old stigma and the fear of being laughed at by their peers, there are hardly a handful who actually visit such institutes!

An honest approach is made to guide the youth and common man to overcome the myths drowning the flames of their lives.

Some sexual myths are busted here by Arvind Minz, Senior Consultant, QRS Hospital, Faridabad.

According to him "They are never helpful and pernicious and mostly we see the teens or youth drowning in these 'myths' leading to a point in their lives which can prove dangerous. 'Healthy Sexual Insight' leads to a healthy life. We cannot deny the importance of sex in our lives".

Sex myths run rampant among teens and youth. Since many teens/youth do not feel comfortable discussing sex with their parents, family doctor, or another trustworthy senior they are more likely to learn their sex facts in the rumour mill.

This is not advisable. There are many half-truths and falsehoods circulating the school halls and if this is where you get most of your information about sex, which you carry up to your college life, you are setting yourself up for disaster.

Sex is seen as a taboo, especially in India. On one hand the mothers wish for their sons and daughters to have a successful, healthy and happy life on the other hand they abstain from guiding them about the most important phenomenon of their lives which eventually helps in forming a family.

Common Sexual Myths:

1. Sexual accomplishments before marriage lead to a successful marital sex life OR inhibited sex life before marriage has a more fruitful effect on marital life.
2. Virginity is essential and non-virgins do not have a successful married life.
3. Pulling out from a woman before ejaculation avoids pregnancy. Men do not always know when ejaculatory fluid begins to seep out - and even ahead of a perceptible orgasm, pre-ejaculate (which includes sperm) is released and is enough to get a woman pregnant..
4. The fourth myth is about the belief that oral sex is safer than vaginal sex. (From teenagers to many powerful ones, oral sex seems to have the stigma of a "free pass" as far as sexual relationships go. Yes, it does count as sex, and yes, you can get a sexually transmitted disease from oral sex.) There is still an exchange of fluids, meaning that diseases can

enter your body through sores or small cuts in your mouth and throat. But oral sex is absolutely normal and not perversion. The most important thing is your bonding with your partner and the respect you have for each other. Having oral sex outside a relationship is not advisable.

5. Another myth is about how certain foods can be aphrodisiacs that will put one in the mood for some good loving. While oysters, dark chocolate, strawberries might make one feel aroused, there is no scientific evidence to support the validity of aphrodisiacs.

6. A serious myth is about how, if all else fails, Viagra and other similar oral medications can treat erectile dysfunction. Oral medications are only a temporary fix to a problem that may have other underlying health causes that should be addressed by a qualified physician. In addition, many men with health conditions, including hypertension and diabetes, cannot take oral prescriptions due to serious potential side effects or contraindications with other medications.

It's easy to be confused about sex. There are so many mixed messages and myths surrounding sex, it can be hard to know what's true and what's not. Before you decide to have sex, it's important that you know the facts.

SEXUAL MYTHS CAN BE SOMETIMES MISLEADING AS THEY CAN LEAD TO SEVERE DEPRESSION AND DEGRADATION OF MENTAL HEALTH WHICH IN TURN LEADS TO FAILURE, NEGATION AND SUICIDE.

Youth becoming a victim of the romour mill simply want to experience sex as without this experience they think themselves to be incompetent.

Let us read about some other Sexual Myths.

Myth a# ORAL SEX is a perversion.

Fact: No it is not a perversion. Oral sex is a matter of choice. If your partner is willing there is no harm in having oral sex but make it safe. Both the partners should be free from diseases.

Myth b# VASECTOMY makes a man impotent.

Fact: Vasectomy makes a man sterile, which means his semen does not contain sperms any more, but this does not mean that he is impotent. He can achieve an erection and have sex as he did earlier. Vasectomy may actually improve his sex life because there is no fear of unwanted pregnancy.

Myth c# A man should be able to achieve an erection whenever he wants to.

Fact: Erection is a response to sexual arousal. One may not be able to attain it at will because of several reasons. Unless the inability to attain an erection prevents a man from having intercourse on multiple occasions it cannot be considered a disorder.

Myth d# Losing one drop of semen is equal to losing about 40 drops of blood.

Fact: Whoever told you this one was probably pulling your leg. Semen is not made of blood. Losing semen is in no way related to losing blood.

Myth e# Having sex with a virgin will cure a man of his venereal disease.

Fact: This is a dangerous misconception. If a man with a venereal disease has sex with a virgin, he will only end up passing it on to her. Effective medicines are available for the treatment of venereal diseases. There is no need to try such baseless and harmful methods.

Myth f# MASTURBATION leads to psychological problems.

Fact: Masturbation does not cause any physical or psychological problems. Anxiety and fear caused by myths about masturbation can cause psychological problems.

Myth g# NOCTURNAL ORGASMS (wet dreams) occur only in men.

Fact: Women may also experience nocturnal orgasms.

Myth h# Wet dreams are a type of sexual disorder.

Fact: It is normal to have wet dreams. They do not indicate a sexual disorder.

Myth i# There is no need to use a birth-control measure during first intercourse.

Fact: One sexual encounter is enough for pregnancy to occur. If you do not wish to conceive, it is extremely important that you use a contraceptive, even for your first intercourse.

Myth j# A man is not a man if he cannot have an erection.

Fact: Erection is just one of the many aspects of a man's sexuality. A man with erectile dysfunction can be absolutely manly in all other ways.

Myth k# A woman is not a woman if she cannot have a child.

Fact: Pregnancy and childbirth are just one of the many aspects of womanhood. Women without children are just as feminine as those without them.

Myth l# Some special foods and exercise can increase the size of the penis.

Fact: No food or exercise can impact penis size. Nutritious food and exercise will improve your overall health, which can improve your sex life.

Myth m# Menopause is the end of a woman's sex life.

Fact: Women cannot conceive after menopause but can continue to have a normal sex life.

Myth n# Sex education leads to promiscuity in young adults.

Fact: This is certainly not a scientifically sound opinion. Sex education can help youngsters have safe and responsible sex. Lack of information from correct channels fuels curiosity and makes them experiment with sex in the wrong manner.

(Thanks to Dr. Arvind Minz, Senior Consultant, QRG Hospital, Faidabad for enlightening us on this topic).

Winning Secret:

- ADVICE AND WARNING: Think you're in-the-know about sex and can weed out fact from fiction. Put your knowledge to the test because we're about to separate fact from fiction and put some sex myths to bed. It's hard to find out the truth about sex, because when we talk about it, we're usually lying.

Must know facts about contraception, pregnancy, sexually transmitted diseases (STDs) and copulation..

It's worth spending a dollar to get some information about sex from a counselor or online counseling from reputed sites before you can really have it.

Sex is just very normal. Don't make it a burden if it happens. Maybe after having you start suffering from the guilt factor (mainly girls) – just do away with it. You are not the only one who has done it. But don't repeat the act for the heck of having it. Respect your relationship.

To have sex has become the most important goal for the youth of today. If one hasn't experienced it during college time, his friends take him as a loser. The pressure to have sex anywhere, sometimes can lead you to miseries. Without being informed you just jump in a hot bowl of soup without any knowledge of the subject and can end up messing up your life with different kinds of sexually transmitted diseases. SO IT IS BETTER TO TALK IT OUT WITH SOMEONE WHOM YOU TRUST OR ANY PSYCHIATRIST. These days online psychiatrists of any reputed site (but do check the site's authenticity) are easily accessible.

Respect your sexual encounters and don't just jump into the pool to prove yourself to be a 'grown up'. You have your entire life. Prepare yourself mentally and be informed positively. This can save you from ruining your life.

[CHAPTER FOURTEEN]

ON A LIGHTER NOTE

HEART IS A TOURIST : MEND BROKEN ONES
HANGOVER OF A BROKEN RELATIONSHIP!

For those youth who think their life is finished with a broken relationship. I am not suggesting to disrespect true love but once when it snaps, many end their lives or sink into pools of depression – Why do they forget, their life is not only theirs but of their parents and well wishers too. So on a lighter note, I have tried to relax their broken hearts and minds!

A relationship is for long but if it is breaking – try saving...but then too if it breaks, do not let it ruin your entire life.

Love is for "loving" not for "languishing". Clinging on to bitterness of past, hangs a slag heap on souls, like "the phantom who never got off King Vikramaditya's back"!

It affects one's mood, attitude, relationship, work status, place in the society and so many important ingredients of life, eating and destroying self-esteem, leading us to the brink of extinction, with "BOUTS OF DEPRESSION!" I DO NOT WANT TO PREACH ANYTHING BECAUSE ONE EXPERIENCING SUCH PHENOMENON CAN NEVER BELIEVE THAT HEART IS A TOURIST!

I AM QUITE SURE, THOUGH IT MAY HAVE SCARS, BUT IT IS NOT THAT IT CAN NEVER EVER BE MENDED.

THE HEART IS A TOURIST... LET IT TOUR....

Actually it is the preconceived conceptions of our minds which does not let our hearts to loiter around the cresses of second or third round of intoxicating pleasures, drawing us away from all the negativity!

NOW PLEASURE HERE DOES NOT MEAN THAT AGAIN YOU WILL LET YOUR HEART MEANDER AROUND OTHER PERSON'S GARDEN!!! uhmm!!!

Forget your past which hurts, but do not let your heart once again want "a forbidden fruit". C 'mon, there are so many opportunities strewn-only one has to waken from his deep slumber and inhale the aroma of tranquilizers around them.

ANGELINA JOLIE'S movie *"THE TOURIST"* is a fine example of it.

"During an impromptu trip to Europe to mend a broken heart, Frank unexpectedly finds himself in a flirtatious encounter with Elise, an extraordinary woman who deliberately crosses his path. Against the breathtaking backdrop of Paris and Venice, their whirlwind romance quickly evolves as they find themselves unwittingly thrust into a deadly game of cat and mouse."

Last evening, my closest friend said, on seeing me little dejected with things happening around, "Nothing is impossible"! We all know this that nothing is impossible but how many of us practice it.

MENDING A BROKEN HEART IS NOT IMPOSSIBLE.. WE ONLY TRY TO RUN AWAY FROM LIFE! SO YOU SEE LIFE IS TO LIVE AND TO LET OTHERS LIVE – MEND BROKEN HEARTS AS FAST AS YOU CAN-USE ANY AND ALL KINDS OF ADHESIVES BUT MEND IT! DO NOT HAVE "EXTREME PREJUDICE" TO JUSTIFY YOUR FEELINGS – SO GET UP-GET GOING!!

HAVE A GOOD TIME AHEAD

[CHAPTER FIFTEEN]

SPECIAL WOMEN'S SECTION

Chapter One:

Who forces a woman to live in an 'abusive relationship' – 'The Society' or 'She Herself?"

Why is 'DIVORCE' A 'DREADED' word?

THE DIVORCE DELUGE ... IS IT REALLY A DRAGON?

For Celebrities and Elite "Divorce was never a big problem"! Moving around with second or even a third partner has never been a debatable issue in their society, especially in India! After the celebrities, it is sometimes, the poorest section of the society which doesn't consider this lacuna of marriage any serious and easily leave their partners and go for the second or third! The

worst sufferer is the INDIAN MIDDLE CLASS and the INDIAN CONSERVATIVE ROYAL GHARANAS!

The royal 'gharanas' too now are to some extent taking divorces lightly as more or less they now, stand, somewhere close to the Elite Modern Class. The worst sufferer, thus, has always been the middle – class!

But somehow it is interesting to note that in the recent years, divorces after all are not looked down upon by the Indian Society, the major share of which is constituted by the middle class. Maybe it is the Consumerist Mentality or Modernisation, but divorces are becoming easier and rampant! As it is said, "we have to pay the price of progress"!

And many psychiatrists too agree. Like, while reading a column I came across, a therapist's viewpoint, that "in the absence of joint families, people don't even know what family and marriage values are. They don't even get time to understand why they are getting married at the first place."

But I think the doctor should understand that, if everything was alright no one would be even requiring the help and views of A RELATIONSHIP THERAPIST! In fact, the more failures – the more treatment and then arises the need of a therapist like him. I wish such therapists were there too to prevent 'Dowry Deaths and Suicides',

This does not mean that I am advocating divorce and nuclear families but the scenario at present in which prices of necessary commodities are touching sky, it is the need of the hour that both the partners work and try to let their relationships work too!

Was it good to hear when earlier women, for false family honour and respect wrapped themselves in a cover of false 'honour' and gave up their lives or is it nice that they are venturing out in the new beckoning world full of promises to save their lives?

Now readers please do not misunderstand me, I do not advocate divorces but then I do not advocate "Dowry Deaths" too! There are circumstances which are trying and testing! But then, I have noticed once again, the children have started valuing their parents, maybe for their selfishness as when both the partners are working, they need them back at home to look after their kids!

Divorce is always not the solution to a "Bad Marriage" and when children are involved it becomes even more serious...

But we all know that RELATIONSHIPS ARE SUCH MATTERS WHERE WE CAN NOT HAVE CUT OUT RULES AND SET FRAME OF MINDS BUT CERTAINLY WE CAN AVOID AND DIMINISH THE DEATH RATES ASSOCIATED TO BAD MARRIAGES – WHEN A LIFE IS SAVED, ONE CAN ALWAYS MAKE IT SUCCESSFUL.

But committing suicide, being burnt to death, crying and wasting one's entire life is no solution either. I know a huge amount of "guilt factor", is also sometimes involved and people are falling into "trap of depression", sometimes after going through the 'Divorce Ordeal!'

Who doesn't want a beautiful relationship? But 'definition of this beauty' is hard to be found. So I think, 'Prevention is better than Cure'. When a disease becomes a tumor, it is better to segregate it from one's body rather than carrying it and eventually meeting the final doom!

Chapter Two:

SUCCESSFUL WOMEN – UNSUCCESSFUL LIFE:

Poets like John Keats have always described nature and humanity in a very enchanting manner. He in fact always tried to create a communion between the two. What I am going to discuss here is totally different from what he or other poets like him might have thought for this Universe. I am going to discuss the Human Mind, its satanic fangs, its rigorous attempt to gain more as well as its brittleness!

MIND OF A MAN is always active and fabricating something. Even in its hibernation, it creates imaginative zones, arenas where it ventures whenever it has time or will to do so.

The incessant suicide rates, murder and deaths of models, celebrities, air-hostesses high profile professionals especially woman has raised a nerve-racking fissure which needs some serious filling. WOMAN, YES WOMAN is mainly becoming victim of the ever-growing HUMAN MIND'S DECAYING NETWORK.

In a bid to achieve more, to have the world swooning round them, sometimes some woman unknowingly start running in the race to 'have more' and when they are not able to achieve this, they end their lives. This is a common occurrence with successful and beautiful ones. In fact they are not able to cope up with the pressures attached to their work and befriend men who do not want anything beyond physical pleasures from them. These men are not committed at all whereas the women never want to let go off them – Now here the traumatic situation begins as every woman at heart is a simple child and wants a mental support in times of their Emotional Breakdown and when they do not get these, they choose to shut their lives and their future, and life is forever doomed.

I sometimes wonder at the Satanic Minds of such Men who know that can never-ever be committed to such ladies due to social pressures, but still make these ladies their "fun-element". And why are these successful women hopeless and unsuccessful in choosing the right partners?

When any death under such circumstances happens, it is generally termed as "Suicide" and forgotten at the next hour as it transpired in India. Viveka Babaji, a very successful model is one such example. She ended up her life and was remembered as a 'news piece' preparing to get stale as fresh news would soon cloud the psyche of the common man. Shouldn't such cases be preserved under 'murder acts?'

Warning And Advice:

I REQUEST ALL MY WOMAN READERS to be strong as not to enter the zone of "brittleness" where their minds can break into pieces, never to be fixed again. I know to preach is very easy and to follow the same very difficult but once the phase is over, then you realise how worthless the person was for whom you were pining!

Choose a profession of your compatibility and where you can handle your relationships as well as emotional traumatising days.

Most importantly, if by chance you have a partner who is already married, try to come out of this relationship as there are very few who would leave their settled lives for 'you', whom they think strong, brave and smart enough to get another boyfriend when they leave you – they would never understand your need – YOU ARE JUST A GLAMOROUS PAST TIME FOR THEM.

AND I ALSO REQUEST ALL THE NEAR AND DEAR ONES OF SUCH VICTIMS TO COME UP FOR THEIR HELP WHENEVER "THEIR FRIENDS NEED THEM".

Chapter Three:

PROMISES ARE MADE TO BE BROKEN

A Warning To All Who Take Promises Seriously......

Coming out of the hospital, Stuti's once beautiful voice would not leave my senses. Her present anxious state and her muffled terrified whispers, echoing in my mind were encircling my steps as though someone was trying to catch me in a rope trap!

How can people be so naive – how can a highly educated woman like her be a mental wreck! Did she not know that nothing is permanent in this world? Why did she then try to end her life? Whom did she want to trust? Her love? Being a literature student, she should have known that fragrance of love evaporates for the materialistic and those who try to linger onto it, drown in a black sea of slimy feelings – yes slimy because those emotions and feelings hold no importance for others except for the person suffering!

Stuti, once a brilliant, beautiful, chirpy girl was now about thirty-five. Ten years back she was married to a respectable boy of her community who was in no way 'respectable' to her! The same story – abuses, bruised body, and butchering mind and soul clung to her marriage. Many a time she tried to come out of the vicious circle but somehow like PREMCHAND'S STORY, *BADE GHAR KI BETI* (Daughter of a renowned family), she too was not able to wade out of the bog of her lame survival!

But the worst thing which she faced was the betrayal of that man who came back into her life, only to shred her into pieces, when she had almost reconciled with her role on this earth!. Ughhh!! "Men", she thought with distaste. Stuti had told her everything – how Vikram resurfaced in her life after fifteen years and promised to be with her always and to my disbelief, Stuti took him literally by his words! Here where a woman goes wrong......

Bad marriage had already tormented Stuti's mind and soul, and when she was almost on her own, a long lost friendship resurfaced only but TO RAPE HER MENTALLY! What had to happen, happened. It ruined and shattered her completely! I badly wanted my friend back into her senses once again – I badly wanted to take her childlike serene face in my hands, waving away parasitic fluffs of childish longing devouring her mind and say, 'PROMISES ARE MADE ONLY TO BE BROKEN...'.

by Phizlina

You promised me you love me,
You promised me you care,
You promised that you'd be here,
But now you're over there,
You promised that you'd be there,
Forever and a day,
You promised I meant the world to you,
But it never was that way,
You promised that I'd have you,
You were always to be mine,
You promised that you'd stay with me
Until the end of time,
You promised that every day,
I will stay in your heart,
You promised that no force on Earth,
Could tear us two apart,
But you left me in the dark,
Made my heart go cold,
For now I know your promises,
Are valueless and old.

Mistakes of Stuti:

1. Mistake :

She bore the abusive relationship without trying to come out of it. Stuti did not try to stand on her own feet, though she was learned and had the right education to her credit. If the same energy applied while bearing the tortures of her husband was applied in carving out a niche for herself, things would have been little better.

2. Mistake:

Stuti did not talk over her problems with others. Talking, discussing and taking help of psychiatrists would have helped her. Many women, just for family and children's sake bear all atrocities committed on them.

3. Mistake:

AND THE MOST GRUESOME MISTAKE: She believed another man who had previously too walked out of her life without any reason!

So I would request all my Woman Readers not to mess up their lives and seal the paths of their survival. Make your life a perennial river which quenches your thirst as well as other's too. I am not saying that we should not trust anyone but 'trusting a person who has earlier ditched' is not advised. Sometimes even the close ones can cheat on you.

If any relationship works, make it work but if it is working on a daily routine basis of 'beatings' and 'abuse', find a way out of it – but before walking out, solidify your grounds. Be smart. Naivety can be dangerous. Wake up and know your rights.

[CHAPTER SIXTEEN]

TRUST: CONFIDENCE: SUCCESS

DISTRUSTING 'TRUST' – A TYRANNY'S DISEASE

The dynamics of trust and distrust are central to understanding modern society. These dynamics are evident at all levels of society – from the child's relation to caregivers to the individual's relation to the state. They span from taken for granted trusting relationships to highly reflective and negotiated contractual interactions. In simple words, our behaviour to a great extent is dependent on our relationship with friends, near-dear ones and acquaintances.

Any negative vibe stains the quotient of trust which we build in our hearts for others. In the present scenario, the mentality of about 40% of people are getting degraded and manipulative, hence it is better too to warn our growing children against the maladies of society, so to prevent them from being trapped emotionally, physically and sexually and from here starts an uneven path of trust… BUT THEN IT IS EVEN MORE NECESSARY TO INCULCATE THE QUOTIENT OF TRUST. The parents on their part are correct but at the same time, they should while quoting examples of grievous nature as the 'sour quotient of warning', should see that an equal amount of 'sweet quotient' too is added in the lives of their children to neutralize the negative effect a child is building towards the society as a whole. This can be so ruinous and a child can forever deform his personality and grow up as a lame youth.

P.S. I do vehemently support parent's action but then at the same time my advice is that they should spend some quality time with their children. As the present time demands both the parents as working, the little time that the parents shed out for their children can actually be rejuvenating for them. Look after their emotional needs, be their friend if not the best one and train them to segregate GOOD from the BAD. Scolding and quoting heinous incidents can make growing children MENTALLY CRIPPLED and they never learn to trust anyone.

Knock… Knock… Cleopatra>success

CLEOPATRA! Yes CLEOPATRA – THE ENIGMA! But what is 'this name' doing here? What is its relevance in a topic of Distrusting Trust and its Repercussions? Isn't she more related to words like 'beauty', 'sex' and 'power'? TRUE! But Wait and Watch.......Have patience to know the 'significance' and 'relevance' of this word here!

'SUCCESS IS A JOURNEY, NOT A DESTINATION', we all know this. The path to success becomes hurdle free and less hazardous if we have the required amount of CONFIDENCE – this is what is generally believed. NOW LET US LEARN SOMETHING INTERESTING BEFORE DIVING INTO "AN OCEAN OF UNKNOWN" TO GAIN CONFIDENCE AND INCULCATING TRUST'...

According to my belief success is somewhat related to "Camaraderie"– a lovely word imparting loveliness to things unnoticed like a tinkling laughter among people! Goodwill and lighthearted rapport – a spirit of familiarity and trust existing between or among friends.

This 'CAMARADERIE' has been responsible for enhancement of CONFIDENCE AND TRUST in so many people who have been friends or care givers!

Advice:

Camaraderie is made from the word COMRADE meaning 'friends' – so we see that the importance of 'friends' and 'friendship' in our lives cannot be evaded, overlooked or ignored.

Friends are those beautiful and selfless people who always GIVE rather 'EXPECT or SNATCH THINGS AWAY' from us. They eclipse the pain of our lives, gifted to us by our NEAR and DEAR ONES, with patches of affection, tolerance, forbearance – their naughty little pranks illumines the gloomy days of our lives! Their wits enhancing and boosting our morale each time they brush with us knowingly or accidently! And in all this, they continually build CONFIDENCE in us, the ancient way – BY GIVING TRUST!

The comrades on the other hand protect us from FOES who like SATAN or BULLIES barge or slyly entwine our lives sucking the essence of it – hence I would like my readers not to confuse a 'comrade' with a 'bully'!

Warning:

A bully can also be your acquaintance or maybe a part of your 'friend circle' but in no case is he your well-wisher. He thrives on the pleasures drawn by thwarting you mentally and physically!

Solution:

WHY PAY BUCKS?

Understanding, faith, trust, affection, selfless love, praise, laughter, joy, healthy competition, feeling of belongingness and many more attributes are there, which contribute to the ingredients of camaraderie.

Now let us come to the topic CONFIDENCE. So much chaos is being added on this simple and pleasant word. People are making egregious mistake by paying 'bucks' to inculcate this 'ingredient' in them forgetting that 'this was always with them' and has never-ever left their side whenever they are or were with their comrade. Have they ever thought of the comfort level in the halo of which they bask when they are sharing their precious moments with their comrades? No. Such trait as 'CONFIDENCE' is required by them to "mingle' and then "tingle"!

Then why is it that a person who mingles so freely bubbling with "CONFIDENCE" in a group of friends becomes meek, gawky and terrified in certain situations? Has anyone ever thought of it? The reason is his taking up the negative comments or situations seriously or fear of the unknown that he might be belittled or berated curbs his genuine and "default confidence quotient". For example: a newlywed, who had been quite a debater in her college lost even her voice after 3-4 years of her marriage due to constant disparaging acts of her husband and her in-laws. The same girl's laughter had once been a life saving act in everyone's life and heart! So we learn that CONFIDENCE CAN BE CREATED

IN A LOVELY WAY IN A LOVELY ENVIRONMENT AND CAN EVEN BE SNATCHED IN DISPARAGING SITUATIONS.

OH MY CLEOPTRA – TEACH THE YOUTH – LEND THEM YOUR TENACITY!!

Advice:

A RISING WAVE ONLY EBBS: DO NOT FEAR FAILURE:

Now let us come to 'one of the most enigmatic character' which is surrounded with a halo of mystery, mystique, beauty, romance, lust and power – CLEOPATRA! She made the world to realize that success comes to those who continually strive for it.

It is true that rising wave ebbs! But why do we forget 'a person who rises can only ebb i.e. no rise-no ebb'! It is a natural phenomenon – a blatant truth. Hence one should not be afraid of failures and downfall.

If Cleopatra would have been afraid of her downfall, Egyptian History would have never ever seemed so enticing and majestic. She was an epitome of CONFIDENCE! Nor did she only symbolize success in Ptolemy Regime but after being jilted, being denied the requisite status by her once, majestic lover, Julius Caesar, and finally him being, assassinated she had three children from her next lover Mark Antony!

She never looked back to lament over the spilled milk neither did she waste time in taking decisions – good or bad!

 # Advice

I am not saying that whatever she did was absolutely correct I am only trying to say that WE SHOULD HAVE FAITH IN OUR ACTIONS AND MOTIVES AND THEN WE SHOULD SURGE AHEAD – INCULCATE FAITH IN OUR SOUL AND SEE HOW CONFIDENCE DEVELOPS BIT BY BIT AND TURNS INTO A BIG POWERFUL TREE FROM A DRY WITHERED SEED – AND YES DO NOT BE AFRAID OF AN 'EBB' AS HE WHO RISES CAN ONLY 'EBB'!

Conclusion:

SUCCESS>CONFIDENCE>TRUST

 # Advice And Winning Trick:

No matter the type of relationship – be it romantic, friendly, or between parent and child, an essential ingredient is trust. Trust defines every interaction in a relationship. It builds intimacy and it strengthens bonds. Without trust no relationship can thrive.

Unfortunately people don't always cherish trust the way they should. Because it is often given freely at first AND is also easily taken for granted. When trust is damaged it can be dangerous for a relationship and once lost it becomes almost impossible to earn it back. SO THOSE BREAKING TRUST SHOULD ALSO THINK HUNDRED TIMES THE CONSEQUENCES OF BACK STABBING.

But somehow this is tyranny's disease, not to trust friends. Let us read what famous philosophers have said about 'TRUST FACTOR' and then try to understand, realize, assess whether we should have faith in our friends - whether we should trust them or not?

Ann Radcliffe in *The Mysteries of Udolpho,* 1764 said "A human being is only interesting if he's in contact with himself. I learned you have to trust yourself, be what you are, and do what you ought to do the way you should do it. You have got to discover you, what you do, and trust it". VERY TRUE – WHATEVER YOU ASPIRE FOR – DO WITH TOTAL DEDICATION. Trust yourself-Have faith in yourself and if you lose, accept it but do not lose courage. Always remember that if one door is closed, there are millions other which are open. You only have to find the key to them!

But my belief is exactly like, Barbra Streisand who in 1942 had expressed and Cardinal de Retz, who had quoted in Memoires:

"Do not trust all men, but trust men of worth; the former course is silly, the latter a mark of prudence".

So we see, we have to TRUST either ourselves or our friends. Every time don't let the fear of being cheated eat you up! I agree people might have cheated upon you and let you down but isn't there faith too which exists at the other side of the dark tunnel - Yes Trust and Faith, which sometimes may get blackened but then it does not mean that you should become a loner and deform your personality! ACCEPT IT GUYS – CHEATING AND CONFIDING, BOTH ARE PARALLEL!

If you do not believe me, believe the famous Thinker, Democritus (460 BC - 370 BC) "Anyone who goes through life trusting people without making sure they are worthy of trust is a fool. Yet there are people who may be trusted, men as well as women. There are as many differences in their natures as there are flowers in these meadows".

ANY HELP: TRUST ME: I AM THERE

[CHAPTER SEVENTEEN]

DRUG ADDICT? ALCOHOL?

NO THEY ARE PORN ADDICTS!

If you suspect you are a pornography addict, or if you are concerned that someone you know may be a porn addict, here is some information that will help.

#About Pornography Addiction

Previously pornography addiction had its roots in the viewing and hoarding of magazine and video cassettes. However, these days porn addicts have new and frighteningly powerful enablers: the Internet, Smartphones, and Social Media.

Porn addicts today can feed their Internet porn problem by viewing online still photos, downloading porn videos, or by having webcam sex (paid and unpaid). Some use the Internet to simply view images while others eventually end up using the Internet as a vehicle to meet with anonymous sexual partners. The 'new media' of smartphones offers some addicts instant phone-based porn downloads along with wherever/whenever live video streaming of sexual activities, while Facebook can leave some cruising images and profiles for hours on end.

MONEY MAKERS ARE USING THE YOUTH MAJORLY TO BLOAT THEIR INCOMES DISPROPORTIONATELY. And what can be better than a 'PORN DIPPED SITE'. A little scope – a nude girl appears and men, especially the youth get deviated.

As I have stated earlier too in 'Sexual Myths' that sex is not bad and we are no saints but our intakes should not surpass our mental metabolism, resulting in mental indigestion.

What is porn addiction?

Similar to someone with a chemical or substance addiction, porn addicts tend to replace important relationships and commitments with their "drug" of choice: pornography.

Non-Internet porn addicts can be found in places like strip clubs and adult bookstores, but it is unlikely that they have a strip club addiction or an adult bookstore addiction, but rather they have consistent and compulsive sexual problems that manifest in different ways.

Effects:

Pornography addicts tend to isolate themselves when engaging in their sexual acting out. They can typically spend many hours or even days lost in two-dimensional images and experiences. Some also lose time to Internet addictions such as online fantasy games and/or gambling sites.

Nonsexual Internet addiction can also be painfully isolating, causing real life consequences for the person addicted to online gambling or fantasy games affecting important love and sex relationships.

While some sex and porn addicts use compulsive masturbation as a part of their acting out, others engage only minimally in the sex act itself but nonetheless end up losing themselves to the endless sexual images and sites found online.

P.S. As I have stated earlier that masturbation is a part of the growing up and a peep into adult sites too but here we are talking about those who constantly hang on these sites, ruining their mental, physical health, financial stability and sometimes become a threat to their very own existence or society – 'RAPE' IS ONE SUCH MALIGNANT GROWTH OF INTERNET PRONOGRAPHY ADDICTION – MAKING MINDS SICK AS THE 'PERVERT SEXUAL ACTS PROVIDED ONLINE IS THE MOST CONTAGIOUS DISEASE'

 # Some signs of porn addiction can include:

- An inability to stop the behaviour(s) and porn use despite previous attempts to do so
- Anger or irritability if asked to stop
- Hiding or attempting to keep secret all or a part of the porn use
- Living a double or secret life related to porn
- Continuing the behaviour despite obvious consequences, such as a relationship or job loss
- Getting lost in the problem porn use (i.e., spending more time than intended, losing time)

 # Combating Porn Addiction:

Recovery from porn addiction requires honesty and outreach. For those addicted to porn and sexual acting out, honesty begins by finding someone knowledgeable working with sexual addiction and admitting the entire problem to them without omitting the embarrassing or humiliating parts.

- The Sexual Recovery Institutes specialize in the treatment of pornography addiction, and offer a confidential assessment to help you move to the next step.

Getting help with porn addiction can feel shameful, embarrassing, or humiliating, but those feelings have to be tolerated when the greater concern is that the pornography addictions will significantly interfere in the life of the sex addict or in the lives of those they love.

The sex addict involved in internet porn addiction often has to arrive at his or her own conclusion to make a change, a decision that often comes a lot later than their partners would like or can tolerate.

 # It's your life: Win It:

Porn addiction help tips

1. Talking about the issues in detail with a trusted friend or therapist who will be as honest with you as you are honest with them.
2. Making an addiction prevention plan to carry out when tempted.
3. Putting tracking devices on your smartphone and computer so others (best not a spouse) can monitor your online behaviour.

4. Knowing the signs of porn addiction, both the general signs and those specific to you.
5. Knowing the stages of porn addiction.
6. Making good use of porn deaddiction resources and recovery support groups available online on authentic sites, as well as sex addiction professionals.

We know very well that Internet has become an essential ingredient of our lives. Not only essential – in today's work from home culture, it has become our daily lifeline.. So in this age of Internet, where almost everything is directly or indirectly related to it, we cannot run away from it – So it is better we refrain from acts which leads to perversion and make the foundation of our lives strong.

Web help from: http://www.theinternetbusinessman.com/dangers-on-the-internet

[CHAPTER EIGHTEEN]

SEX, CITY, SCAVENGERS AND INTERPERSONAL SKILLS

MAKING MOUNTAIN OUT OF A MOLE – INTERPERSONAL SKILLS. "WHAT IS IT"?

My Readers would definitely wonder what actually has happened to me and what exactly the topic holds for them! "WHAT A VOLATILE TOPIC IT IS? Would it be worth reading?" To them I would like to say, "give it a read, then form your opinion."

Lexicons, people and hundreds of different websites daily come up with different expressions, meanings and audio-visuals of Interpersonal Skills! So many meanings–enough to leave anyone baffled, confused, perplexed amazed and leading them after all nowhere!

Whenever I am asked to speak on this topic I simply laugh it off or resort to some musings which might not at all be serious at times!

Communicatingeffectively,convincingly,charismatically oozing with self-confidence has become the latest trend which gives the requisite lift to our "LIFESTYLES" though it can however, sometimes put off the listeners! BUT SIMPLY TO BE IN THE CIRCLES OF LITERATES "they" wear an intelligent look on "their" faces!!! What not has been said and done but the stark naked truth is that even I sometimes though unwillingly, have resorted to "hardcore professional terms" with "worksheets", "feedback forms",etc.

Now let us come to a "profession" which has been eyed with suspicion and negativity but which is using this skill so deftly from ages and ages to get millions of visitors daily! Though previously "they" were mostly illiterate in the said profession due to their "birth factor" or were forcibly pushed into it!

With the passage of time however the scenario has changed. Then they were called "prostitutes" – after a little while "sex workers" and now of course "Escorts" – Giving "style" and "oomph" to the same work, say modernizing the same element!!! Or one can say packaging the age-old ingredient in a more vibrant, tantalizing, illuminating "wrap"!!!!

It can be said that "they" have even superseded "Management Gurus" in their "trade"! If this is the trade they have been taught, forced into or chose on their free will – At least they have been honest enough to show the whole world their brilliancy in it! They have generated or catered to the needs of UNLIMITED SCAVENGERS IN UNLIMITED CITIES from Las Vegas to Portugal, Mumbai, Kolkata and to many more glittering cities – cities that never sleep – cities which go on with its style, fashion, affluence, oomph and few of us are trying to inculcate "interpersonal skills" –a skill that is gifted to "them" most naturally. It was even before the age of concrete communication like postcards, telegrams, cellphones, internet, emails, fax etc. But nobody tried to learn this art from them as most of the time they were and are treated as malignant cell of the society and our bureaucrats, politicians, news channels and other eminent people DURING THE DAY TIME were and are wasting their time and energy to eradicate them from the society lest they would become cancerous! HOWEVER IN THE NIGHT, THE STORY HAS ALWAYS BEEN DIFFERENT!!! Many times "such people" have been caught red-handed enjoying "their" companies unashamedly to their fullest!

Whether all this is a crime or not I'm no one to decide! CRIME is when such people run away from this NAKED TRUTH during day time and don't delve deeper into the pain or the source of the pain, of the people involved in this "trade" which have brought them into this business.

Advice and Winning Tricks:

Sex sells and will sell, no one can stop or do anything about it. The age-old "taboo" has millions of buyers every day and every night! But this doesn't mean that I am agreeing to this network which at times is murky, gloomy, pervert, abusive and filled with lechers or rather SCAVENGERS who are ready to tear apart the soul and body of anyone – yes I mean anyone. For such SCAVENGERS "perversion" is their religion! Hence society as a whole has to be extra attentive of these SCAVENGERS as anytime "this pervert network" can show its venomous fangs and sting innocent people on the name of cleaning dirt from the society, by implicating false charges on them – AFTER ALL, THEY ARE SCAVENGERS, AREN'T THEY"? So you see how the network works! Before anyone close to you knowingly or unknowingly falls into this heinous, murky trap – get alert!!

Here I would like to applaud INDIAN GOVERNMENT WHICH TOO HAS COME TO TERMS WITH AGE-OLD TABOO "SEX" – THAT IS WHY SAFE SEX HAS

BECOME AN IMPORTANT FEATURE IN THE RECENT CURRICULUM OF CBSE BOARD EXAMINATIONS "IN LIFE SKILLS" section and it is better for the parents too, to come to terms with it and develop a better communication with their children and inculcate positive values.

To Err is Human :

Reverting once again to the ongoing topic, I do not want to malign anyone or mention anyone's name here but my readers would definitely be aware of many such PEOPLE.

I, however cannot stop myself from mentioning a name selling like hot cake couple of years back – TIGER WOODS – BUT I REALLY ADMIRE HIM!! THE WAY HE HAD TAKEN UP EVERY THING IN HIS STRIDE WAS COMMENDABLE! Every human being in his or her life at times gets drifted or allured! Don't we know, "to err is human". One whose "acts" are out is a philanderer, coquette or a culprit and one whose follies are tightly secured in a sealed "ALLADIN'S GINNIE'S BOTTLE" is a "saint"!

Actually I must say Woods's Interpersonal Skill IS WEAK!!!! Or he realised, SILENCE IS THE BEST CURE! As sometimes silence holds more importance than "eloquence"! THE LADIES, HOWEVER, TURNED OUT TO BE SMARTER IN THIS ENTIRE EPISODE!!!They made money like hell. In fact his divorce too is up till now the "costliest"! The recent news, however is that Woods's wife is calling off the divorce – This is yet to be revealed!

But is anybody speaking about the million dollars he has donated to the earthquake victims of Haiti!!!If at all someone speaks, he/she will say surely that he did this only to cover up his image and make it straight!!!Imagine a wife not wanting to touch her husband but willing to touch or rather grab his million dollars after divorce! Now this is my view – I do not want anyone to abide by or agree to it. One thing which I like most about my country is "Freedom of Speech and Expression" which has made me to sit at my desk and put up my views so freely!

Talking of Interpersonal skills, let us take a more simpler example of renowned characters "BRUTUS" and "ANTONY" from Shakespeare's JULIUS CAESAR. Can anybody deny Antony's charisma of oratory and convincing power? He was so impressive that his speeches not only made the Romans to go against their "idol", Brutus but the mob themselves set their CITY Rome ablaze, threw their own children in fire but avenged Caesar's death and "fall"! Did Antony ever visit any "coaching centre" to learn "oratory skills – correct choice of words and refrains", which even defeated the legend "Brutus's views" who was held in high esteem by the Romans? Caesar's death was avenged by a mesh of powerful words used correctly and timely by Antony whose tongue worked as fuel in inflaming and instigating the mob.

Now let us keep away all examples. Shouldn't Interpersonal skill be cultivated with little efforts with one's own strong will? I am not suggesting that one should not take help of Trainers, Coaches, Teachers but unless one has the grit, will power and enthusiasm to try, no one can hone or polish their skills – not even the person best at it! And once Interpersonal skill is shown – courage comes naturally – courage to brave and fight against all odds and evens in life.....enough courage to show these scavengers their real and true colours. Shouldn't we all join hands and vehemently oppose the SCAVENGERS who slyly and cunningly flourish in our cities under false cover of respectable persons!

Sex, City and Scavengers:

So we see how SEX in our CITIES is flourishing and SCAVENGERS are roaming about freely – without fear! So it is high time now that we should come to "certain terms" and be comfortable and make others comfortable respectively. AND YES SCAVENGERS ARE NOT GENDER RESTRICTED – A WOMAN TOO COULD BE INVOLVED IN THE WHOLE NETWORK – SO COME TO YOUR SENSES, AWAKEN YOUR MIND, BODY, SOUL AND FIGHT AGAINST IT!

[CHAPTER NINETEEN]

EMOTIONAL COMPASSION VERSUS UNKNOWN ABUSES

What are We Really Doing?

Being "HUMAN" is not enough – One has to become "HUMANE" to have eyes which can see in every winter night, the biting cold and chilling wind lurking slyly comes as a messenger of death, to those sleeping on footpaths, parks, and under any half-constructed building or a tree clutching tightly a stray dog for warmth who is more compassionate than any other rich man swirling past in their big cars, gifting a dusty cover!

For these underprivileged ones, life means more than hygiene…more than those bill boards mocking at the whole system to keep the environment free of certain diseases! This is INDIA…didn't they know when they were putting up such ironical hoardings!

C'mon,"They" knew very well but a kind of system has to be devised – a system has to exist but how much we all get out of it is a mystery and definitely history will stand to vouch for the same! Overburdened with poverty sharing meals with dogs and cat is a stark naked truth of the 'wretched poor' of this country. Many want to shy away from this reality whilst some USE, very effectively and cleverly "this state of deprivation" to make their "fat" purse "fatter"!

Looking at the 'skyscrapers' one wonders, "Are the so called EMPIRES, of so many GREEDY PEOPLE really a thing to be reveled at?" Probably, Yes, because development is inevitable, incessant and necessary.

Moreover hasn't a Renowned Philospher, Herbert Spencer quoted "Survival of the fittest" i.e. he only survives who is fit and is able to win the race of life, say like snakes which eats most of its own eggs after laying....Now we have to think... Do we want ourselves to be identified with such cold-blooded animals or a warm-blooded human being? Which once again, another acclaimed Thinker, Aristotle has quoted as a "Rational Animal". I do not want to challenge their statements but isn't it ironical how a Rational Animal can survive and be the fittest because one who is "rational" at times will definitely be "Emotional" as he would possess "a brain" and not "a mechanized instrument" in his skull. I guarantee a man with a "throbbing brain" has to be emotional at times and an "Emotional Man" can never survive amongst the Snakes. His emotions unknowingly and accidentally will turn out to be such follies which will take shapes of rock-sized obstructions in the path of the "said progress"!

The other day while watching television, wrapped comfortably in my quilt, sipping coffee and waiting for the arrival of New Year 2011, I could not help thinking about those millions who might not even know "what a new year is"? For them EVERY DAY AND EVERY NIGHT is a race to be alive....the "survival of the fittest". HAVEN'T THEY TOO DEVISED MEANS TO SURVIVE ON "THIS BEAUTIFUL PLANET" with "BEAUTIFUL PEOPLE MASTERING AMAZING TONGUE TWISTERS"!This indeed is a slap on the face of all those who claim to be "humane" and close to "humanity" and that includes probably ME TOO! Sitting comfortably and thinking about the underprivileged is an easy way to show compassion but to venture out to lend a helping hand, in the biting cold with equally cold screeching wind is TRUE COMPASSION.

I do not want to be a "PHILOSOPHICAL GURU" and chide the human race, I only want a few drops of nectar in the form of compassion and affection for those who do not know the real meaning of being a HUMAN BEING...those sometimes hugging animals are closer to compassion and humanity than "those who sit in palatial buildings and formulate plans for such people".

The other day while taking my routine morning walk at about 6:30 a.m., I saw three children (refer to the photograph below), all girls aged about seven, five and one. I could not stop myself from asking their names because in this chilling cold, the elder one named "JYOTI" was carrying the youngest named "ANCHAL". Again this was a dire case of IRONY because Anchal means warm soothing covering of a woman's dress and here this 'anchal' to the youngest was provided by a seven-year-old tender aged child who herself needed love, care and affection!!They were all sisters and the middle one, named "KAJAL" informed that since their mother had to go early in the morning to "Kothis" for odd works like cleaning, washing utensils, etc, they had to look after their baby sister.

I felt ashamed of myself and I knew why.... because without engaging a domestic help even our lives do not run smoothly and we hardly are bothered to look at the stream of pain flowing beyond our luxury and comforts. Wasn't this again a slap on the face of our system and government which puts hoardings 'banning child labour' and under the same hoardings such children like JYOTI either directly or indirectly are taking shelter from different shades of life!

I am not here to force my "thoughts" or "views" on anybody. I wrote what I felt – what my soul wanted to write.....'Selfishness' is a human trait, present in everyone of us. But isn't 'compassion' too an inherent quality gifted to us naturally which we have unashamedly hidden under a quilt of MATERIALISM! What really is needed are "A few drops of compassionate nectar" and the entire race of all behaviors would come to peace!

[CHAPTER TWENTY]

DECISION MAKING

THE MOST IMPORTANT INGREDIENT OF SUCCESS

Decision Making is not a child's play and many significant writers and renowned people have presented their dissertations on the said topic involving lots of tongue-twisters and words which generally overflow the minds of common people. Here I have tried to highlight its importance in a simple manner which would surely help the readers.

The functional area of Decision Making is wide and has seen its vital place in World Wars, appeasement treaties, Economic Recessions and crises to release of movies, deciding schools for children, buying or not buying a car or house at a certain time and many more other areas which may at times seem insignificant but has immense

impact on our lives. Here I am reminded of the novel Name Of Rose by Umberto Eco published in 1980. Initially the publishers had expected its sale up to 3000 copies but in total 10 million copies of it was sold after publication. In US itself about 2 million copies were sold! The success of the novel is till now, a mystery to the publishers as well as to the author himself. Eco says probably it was the right time, when the novel was published – had it been published ten years before or ten years after, it would have BOMBED! So knowingly or unknowingly Eco's and the publishers decision to publish the novel at that particular time span was responsible for its overwhelming success! So, here, the correct timing was in a way responsible for the success of the novel.

As we all know there are many key factors which mould our decisions – these are situations, circumstances, incidents, grooming, wealth, right values and many more. Decision-making is a tough job even if it is made at such levels as to what dress should be worn by one at a certain place or function. It involves a meticulous analysis of all possible opportunities i.e. dresses and accessories available at that time.

My readers must be surprised to see me dealing with topics like EMOTIONAL ABUSE AND DECISION MAKING AT THE SAME BREATH. To them I would like to convey that I am not deviating. In fact I am coming to it – what I am trying to bring out is the point that in situations of such abuses too, one has to take stern and immediate decisions, instead of dilly-dallying and finally coming to an undesirable end. If the person, here, chooses to stay with the abuser he/she should inculcate in himself enough mettle to brave all kinds of situations and make a recognizable place for himself in the society. This however is extremely difficult as constant berating hampers the confidence and the person feels "good for nothing."

Winner's Guide:

Hence to go ahead in life positively, one has to take the decision of his life within time. In doing so he might become an object of 'jest' but this is much better than leading a mentally paralytic life! In fact such decisions enhances the confidence of the person striving to come out of undesirable circumstances, and ENRICHES his personality.

Correct decision at the correct time without being confused, bewildered, matters a lot.

Such clear decisions can only make one to move ahead in life despite of all kinds of obstacles and hurdles. Sometimes some decision can be risky too and requires lot of courage and positivity. In such cases right attitude, acumen and insight is needed and sometimes a DISCUSSION on the matter too helps. So before taking the BIG LEAP one should always organise his valid points WITHIN TIME and then proceed. As Robert Frost has beautifully said, "Two roads diverged in a wood, and I....I took the one less traveled by, and that made all the difference....".

EPILOGUE

REALISATION....

Going for my routine puja of "Thursday" I found the world so beautiful…God always be there with us....And with them who stay in our hearts...near or far!

The Huge Peepal and The Banyan tree, while moving around them taught me the hidden meaning of life.

I touched, sensed, felt their huge magnanimity and benevolence....so many people offering them the religious offerings often not required by them... but still they accept without any complaints...

The trees taught me to be patient, calm and composed in moments of crises… accepting whatever comes your way but not letting it harm you....AND ALSO TAUGHT TO ACCEPT SWEETS WITH LOVE BUT NOT TO LET IT HARM YOU...

Few lines of Rudyard Kipling from the poem *"If"* really helped ....

"If you can keep your head when all about you
Are losing theirs and blaming it on you;

....

If you can trust yourself when all men doubt you,
But make allowance for their doubting too;

....

If you can wait and not be tired by waiting,

....

If you can dream-and not make dream your master;
If you can think-and not make thoughts your aim......"

HAVE A HAPPY LIFE AHEAD.